The Savvy Entrepreneur's
BUSINESS HANDBOOK

A strategic guide to fundraising, networking, market fit and more

Written By Tallis Salamatian MBA

Published by Tallis Salamatian

2020

The Savvy Entrepreneur's

BUSINESS HANDBOOK

A strategic guide to fundraising, networking, market fit and more

By Tallis Salamatian, MBA

Copyright © 2020 by Tallis Salamatian

All rights reserved. This book or any portion thereof may not be reproduced or used in any manner whatsoever without the express written permission of the publisher except for the use of brief quotations in a book review or scholarly journal.

First Printing: 2020

ISBN 978-1-7923-2979-1

Published by:

Tallis Salamatian
201 Coffman St. #1353
Longmont, CO 80501

www.tallis.co

For my Father, Mostafa Salamatian

When I was young my father told me:
"A smart man learns from his mistakes and
a wise man learns from others."

This is my attempt to convey the lessons I've
learned and the wisdom I'd like to share.

Table of Contents

Table of Contents	7
Purpose	8
Coming Up with an Idea	11
Talking	16
Building the Team	25
The real Art of the Deal...	32
Marketing	44
Your First Investor	55
What Investors Want	59
Alternative Funding Sources	82
What I've Learned	87
Entrepreneur's Checklist	101
Glossary	104
Acknowledgements	113
Author Bio	114

Purpose

I've been lucky to have had great mentors and teachers who have taught me countless lessons throughout my 15 years of business experience. My father was a businessman and I was able to learn a lot from his business interactions. More importantly, he supported and funded my early, unsuccessful ventures. Without his and my mother's support I would never have had the opportunity to start my early ventures and would not be where I am today.

When I was young, my father told me:

"A smart man learns from his mistakes and a wise man learns from others."

This is my attempt to impart the lessons I've learned and the wisdom I'd like to share.

I've read books that spend an entire chapter going over relatively simple concepts, I don't want to do that. I have, in fact, covered many of these key concepts while teaching an entrepreneurial course at University of Colorado Boulder's Leeds School of Business.

I am dyslexic so it takes me about ten minutes to read a single page, and I don't have time to sit and spend hours reading. I suspect I'm not the only one, so rather than be long-winded, I'm going to try to keep things to the point.

I'll start off with talking about how important networking is and I'll share stories about how I've benefited from the many connections I've made with people throughout my life. Having these connections will be critical in building your future team and securing funds.

Then I'll go to the core of the book, which is basically a crash course of what I think you should know when starting your business.

1. CONCEPT
   The process of coming up with a start-up concept and the three main types of start-up ideas

2. NETWORKING
   Best practices for networking and making the most of every encounter

3. TEAM BUILDING
   Building a team and who you'll need to take your idea into reality

4. FINANCE
   Breaking down equity and voting rights of shares — this is important to understand when putting your team together and planning a fundraising strategy

5. MARKETING
   Making sure your product is a match for the market you're targeting

6. **FUNDRAISING**
   Finding your initial investment to get going

7. **LESSONS**
   Lessons I've learned through my journeys in entrepreneurship

I finish the book off with a checklist for you to start your business. I hope you benefit from and enjoy my stories and experiences I've gained throughout my 15 years in entrepreneurship.

Coming Up with an Idea

How does someone come up with a start-up idea? What type of divine inspiration does it take to come up with the next billion dollar venture?

There are three main ways to come up with a company idea: 1) Look for a market inefficiency and provide a solution to fix the market inefficiency, 2) Identify a product or service that needs improvement and look for ways to solve that issue, 3) Invent a novel technological advancement. I've been involved with all three types of companies.

1) Market Inefficiency: When there is a supply of something, be it physical or digital, and there is a demand for that thing, but for some reason the people who want it can't get it easily.

2) Optimization: If something irritates you it will probably irritate others, too. If you can find a way to simplify a process or make life easier, you've got something there. To use a cliche, build a better mouse trap.

3) Scientific Breakthrough: If you're an engineer, scientist, tinkerer or genius and you've come up with an innovative product or solution.

My first venture is a great example of identifying a market inefficiency opportunity. In 2001, when iTunes came out, I realized that I wasn't the only one who had figured out that many people were willing to buy MP3s, despite their lower quality.

However, there was a problem with the initial iTunes model: They focused only on mainstream artists. Around this same time, home recording studios had become inexpensive enough for people to start recording their own music at home. Combine this with WAV format trending toward MP3 and the fact that professional studio recordings and well-mastered home recordings were becoming comparable.

At the time, the main way independent artists sold music was through a company called CD Baby, essentially a CD drop shipping service. There was no market-dominant digital platform for independent artists comparable to what iTunes had with mainstream artists; thus a market inefficiency was born.

I started Too Much New Music in 2004 to address the market inefficiency in the independent music market. I ran into several issues along the way that taught me many lessons. I was too inexperienced and didn't yet know the things I would learn during my MBA program. And the venture was too early. I tried to get music labels to invest, but they didn't see the end of the CD coming yet. SoundCloud, an online platform that tried to fix the market inefficiency, didn't become popular until 2008.

Another company I started, called BaziFIT, is also a market inefficiency play, disguised as a fitness app. BaziFIT is a platform that walks users through workouts from their favorite social media fitness personality and tracks performance with feedback via the BaziFIT app and sensor.

There were a few things that I saw in the fitness space that stood out. First, everything on the market is focused on heart rate or steps, and that isn't the best measure of exercise performance. To provide a better measuring instrument, we designed a tool to not only count reps, but also give feedback on form.

I also saw that social media fitness influencers have a ton of engaged followers, but they try to monetize their audience by selling them supplements or clothes. Some trainers have also invested in video content DVDs or apps to distribute their videos. The problem is that you can't generally work out in a gym while following along with a video. Essentially, there was no platform for the scalable dissemination of workout content that also tracked that client's progress over time. So we created a platform that does just that.

This next example is of something that pisses you off. I was brought onto a project by the founder, who, interestingly enough, I just so happened to meet on an airplane. He specializes in laparoscopic surgery (where they inflate your abdomen and perform the surgery via small porthole incisions rather than slicing you all the way open) and he was irritated that while performing surgery it was difficult see what he was doing because of the abundance of blood in the surgical area.

Prior to his invention, the primary method of removing blood from the surgical area was via sponge or suction tube. Sponges are the number one object left behind after surgery, accounting for hundreds of millions of dollars in malpractice suits. Additionally, when you remove the sponge from the porthole, the liquid is rung out back into the body.

Conversely, anyone who's been to the dentist knows that a suction tube sucks indiscriminately and can get stuck on surrounding tissue. Your cheek is one thing but you don't want that on your liver or other organs.

In response to this agitation of choice, the surgeon invented and patented a sponge/tube hybrid; essentially a sponge with a tube in the middle. This solves for multiple problems: The sponge is tethered to the tube so it can't be left behind, the sponge never gets fully saturated because the tube is evacuating the liquid and the suction is passive, thus being gentle on surrounding tissues.

My friend the surgeon identified the problem in his everyday life, then found a simple solution. Many of you reading this might think well, duh, any idiot could have figured that out, but for decades nobody took the initiative to put two objects that are ubiquitous in surgery together to make them both infinitely more effective. Just because an idea may sound simple doesn't mean it can't also be highly effective, even life saving. The simplest ideas often yield the greatest results.

My final example is of the technological ingenuity sort from my favorite of the companies, Nu Promethean Technologies. The founder and brilliant inventor behind this technology realized that he had discovered a way to manipulate graphene into any shape he wanted. This technology has the potential to revolutionize the way we make batteries, power generators, electronics and more. With no exaggeration I can say that this technology, once fully developed, will change the world. Granted, most start-ups will not be in this category, but it is possible and, while rare, these inventions provide a paradigm shift, allowing for massive technological gains. If you do feel your idea fits into this category, talk to a patent attorney. You do not want to make a public disclosure, making your idea public domain ... or do you?

Don't worry, you won't get it right on the first try; it's all about iteration. I don't know of any company that hit a home run in their first at bat of starting a company. There are going to be pivots and constant iteration to improve the concept. As an entrepreneur you must use the scientific process. Come up with a hypothesis (your business model or product), test it, improve and repeat, even after people are willing to buy it.

In summary there are three main ways to start a business and every business is different.

1. Find and fix a market inefficiency.
2. Fix an imperfect product or experience that impacts a segment of the population.
3. Create a purely new technological invention or innovation.

Talking

Before I get into the meat and potatoes of physically starting your business, I'd like to talk for a minute about ... talking! Communication skills, being able to carry an intriguing and interesting conversation, is one of the most powerful weapons you can possess as an entrepreneur.

As an entrepreneur you are constantly talking to people. Recruiting team members, cultivating investors and networking all require exceptional communication skills. This isn't just the ability to effectively convey a message, you need to be likable and enjoyable to talk to. The way to do this is to be genuinely inquisitive and interested in the person you're speaking with.

One of the most important skills I possess is the ability to communicate with people. From a young age I've been driven to speak to people; everyone, really. This drive to communicate is so strong, I'd call it an urge or compulsion. This compulsion has afforded me the opportunity to speak with some truly exceptional people, like Donald Rumsfeld, and talking to people has also helped me get out of binds.

Growing up as an only child, my parents were able to spend all their time and resources on me. The problem was I had a lot of toys, but nobody to play with, so it encouraged me to make friends, which thankfully I was good at. This proved to be a useful skill as I went to three elementary schools and two junior high schools. It was also very useful when moving from California to Massachusetts to Colorado.

The way I see it, almost everyone has something interesting about them, and I really enjoy the search and discovery of what that is for each person. Any new insight you can gather furthers your own overall knowledge, so you should never deny yourself that window of opportunity.

Sure, when I was young we didn't have smart phones, so people were a lot easier to talk to. But I've also noticed that a good conversation is worth more today because of our current insularity. Have you ever looked around and noticed that you're the only person not looking at a screen?

If someone told you that the next person you bump into will give you the secret to success, I bet you'd engage that person and try to draw out that answer. The problem is that there is no one person that can offer that, and if they do you surely won't know before speaking with them. The following are situations where speaking or being approachable has directly benefited me.

My father and I have always been massive soccer fans. He took me to the 2006 World Cup in Germany where we attended several games, including Iran vs. Angola, Ukraine vs. Saudi Arabia and Germany vs. Portugal. Those are some of my most cherished memories. After the tournament ended I backpacked through Europe for the rest of July and through August. This was pre-iPhone so was using actual paper maps. I sent e-mails home every few days to make sure my folks knew I was OK. I met and was hosted by many amazing people through my travels in Europe.

One instance of a chance meeting that stands out began when I was traveling through Germany. I met a British guy who said I could crash with him for a few days in Manchester, but when I got to Manchester and gave him a call — no answer. Great. So I went to an ATM to withdraw cash and it didn't work. I went to the bank and discovered that in the UK, credit card and debit card transactions needed to be done with cards that have chips in them. This was in 2006, 10 years before the United States would start implementing these same cards.

At the time I was absolutely stranded. I had been using my cash up to that point and was planning on using my card from then on because I didn't want to get my cash stolen. Feeling defeated, I went to a bar and watched the Manchester United game. After the game, cricket came on the tube. I went up to the bar and spent my last five quid on a pint and turned to the man next to me to ask him to explain the game of cricket to me. After we chatted a bit I told him my situation and he offered to host me. I stayed at his house for four days while I got my finances situated.

I would have been sleeping on the street in Manchester if I hadn't connected with my now friend, Sean. Instead of moping around being broke I decided to make the best of the moment and get to know the guy sitting next to me. I had no intention of asking him for a place to stay; I was just genuinely enjoying the moment and conversation. Thinking back, this is a good example of making a personal connection with people without motive or preconception. Sean and his buddy, Jamie, who I spent those four days with, came to visit me in California for a couple weeks the following year.

Another distinctive meeting happened my senior year of high school. I tore my ACL, MCL and meniscus playing soccer. This was the first of a total of four knee surgeries, three of them done by my now friend, Dr. Chris Lehman. After my fourth surgery in 2013, I asked him how I was supposed to track my incremental improvements and when I'd be able to play soccer again. He said there was no way of knowing exactly and that it was a process. This wasn't a good enough explanation for me so I continued the discussion with him and we ended up founding BaziFIT together to track progress while working out.

After attending a capstone seminar in Greece during my MBA program, my parents gave me an early graduation gift: a week on the Greek island of Crete. On my way back to Athens to catch my flight home I sat next to a gentleman who looked exactly like the Dos Equis "Most Interesting Man in the World," (it wasn't him). The man turned out to be the head of the biophysics department at the University of Patras and we began chatting. During the one-hour flight we covered a number of topics, including my idea for BaziFIT and the concept of tracking workouts and recovery progress. He suggested that we needed a sensor to better and more accurately track progress. I replied that I was an MBA and had no idea how to make a device that did what he was suggesting. He said not to worry, that he'd build the device for me. Him and his team did, and the device is awesome.

Beyond my personal examples of how talking to people has literally put food on my plate and a roof over my head, the number one reason an investor puts money in a company is a personal connection with the founder. The sad truth is that unless you are in a situation that allows you to truly bootstrap, you will more than likely need capital resources. Check out Crunchbase.com and you'll see that most successful start-ups had $500,000 to $1 million in seed stage funding. Funding at this stage is typically through connections because of the risk profile, and connections are gained and maintained with communication.

If you're a networking superstar then please skip to the next chapter. The rest of this chapter is devoted to those who don't have an easy time talking to strangers.

Some have asked me: How do you just strike up a conversation with someone? The answer is as different as the people you're talking to. It depends on who the person is that you want to talk to, and it depends on where you are. Stopping a busy parent at the grocery store is not the best way to strike up a conversation. The most important thing is to make sure you have enough time to have a relatively full conversation, based on the situation. I've found that the easiest time to start a conversation is when people are waiting around for something, like at an airport or in a long line.

The simplest way to start is to bring up a shared experience. It could be about the weather, local sports teams, or it could simply be about a crazy person yelling at themselves on the street.

Another way to connect with a person is via observation. I speak several languages at a basic level, and a handful of phrases in about 10 different languages. It is amazing how far "please," "thank you" and "cheers" can take you in starting a conversation. Putting the effort into learning at least that much will not go unnoticed. I also read *The Economist* and stay up to date with current events around the globe. This way, when I meet someone who is foreign, I usually know at least a little about their home nation. This rarely goes unnoticed.

Once you have a response and eye contact you can, based on their response, say something to begin a conversation.

You: [Make a comment about a shared experience] "Looks like the charging port between the seats isn't working."

Other person: [Gives an affirmation to your comment] "Yeah, that is unfortunate."

You: [Make another observation and pose it as a question] "Nice suit, are you a lawyer?"

Other person: [Becomes more interested] "No, ha. I'm the COO of a global shipping company."

You: [Continue the conversation] "Very cool, what do you think about the proposed Tesla cargo ships?"

Other person: [Is now engaged in the conversation] "That's interesting, I haven't heard of them yet. What have you heard?"

I'd highly recommend keeping up with current events and learning a few phrases in as many languages as you can. Sports teams are another easy way to connect with people: European soccer clubs, NFL, NBA, MLB, NHL and NCAA are all leagues that if you're familiar with can help you engage in conversations with people.

OK, I'm trying to keep it 100. When striking up a conversation never say anything remotely inappropriate. If the person is in any way not receptive then it's best to not push it. The last thing you want is to have someone think you are hitting on them or that you're a creep.

I'd like to discuss a couple of common places I've met interesting people. I admit I often do my best networking when I'm alone. My wife hates it when we are out together on a date and I start chatting with some random people.

Airports and Airplanes

When you're traveling you often have people sitting next to you. This is a great opportunity to strike up conversations with people. The trick is to start the conversation early because once people pop in their headphones you've lost your opportunity. I've met dozens of very interesting people when I sat next to them on flights.

TSA lines are a good place to meet people. You can strike up a conversation while getting in line by making a comment about how long or short the line is. For example, I was traveling a few weeks ago and there was construction at Denver International

Airport and the TSA at the main checkpoint was directing people to the checkpoint at the other end of the airport saying the lines were much shorter. So I followed their instructions and headed to the other line. Once I got there I found a longer line with less agents to process people. I turned to the guy next to me and said, "Man! I should have just stayed at the other TSA line." The guy next to me said "I know right, they told me to come here, too." After hearing us have this exchange the guy ahead of me turned around and said TSA told him that as well. We then had a nice chat through the line. One was a physicist from Toronto who told me about an interesting article that was in the field of one of my ventures.

Bars or Networking Mixers

When I'm networking I will have a drink but nurse it. Sometimes I'll have a gin and tonic and have the bartender refill my drink with tonic when I'm halfway done.

The best networking is done before people get drunk. Avoid trying to talk business if you're too many drinks deep. People respect restraint and knowing one's own limits.

If you want to approach someone who is speaking with someone else, wait for a lull in the conversation and chime in on the topic being discussed with something notable to add, or find a segue into what you want to discuss.

End the conversation on a high note and don't linger. If you are having a good discussion, set up a time to follow-up over coffee.

The knowledge and wisdom I have gained from these seemingly random interactions have helped immensely in my development as an entrepreneur, as well as my own personal development. Talk to as many people as you can because you never know who you may meet and who can help you. Every person you meet is a potential person who can help your company. You'll never know for sure until you talk to them.

Building the Team

There are countless adages about the importance of a good team, so I'll spare you the cliché. I will say that for every person that you have on your team, assuming you have good team members, your project is stronger and better off.

Don't worry, you don't need to be an engineer or programmer to start a company, but it does help. In my experience there are several key positions that you need to have filled before you can get serious. These roles don't need to be individual people; there can be overlap. Ideally you'd want specialization for the majority of the team.

1) CEO

    The CEO is the visionary for the company and the builder of the team. They lead the team, provide strategic vision and fundraise. If the team doesn't include a CFO and COO the CEO typically becomes responsible for CFO activities and sometimes COO activities.

2) CTO

    The CTO is in charge of all things technical. If there is no COO, the CTO sometimes takes on those responsibilities. Whether you're a software or hardware company or even a hair salon, you need technology to excel in today's economy. A salon may just need someone familiar with graphic and web design, whereas a tech company may need a wider range of talent based on specific needs. These skills include electrical engineerings, mechanical engineering, app developing, web developing, data science, Artificial Reality / Virtual Reality and Artificial Intelligence / Machine Learning.

3) **CFO**

Having an advisor or team member proficient in finance is critical to raising funds. He or she will need to help create projections (pro forma calculations) via spreadsheet that outline your burn rate (how much you're spending per month), identifying your capital expenditure and operating expenditures. This spreadsheet will help you determine the amount of funds you'll need and the allocation of those funds. This is an important job and can be a hard one to fill; I've been asked countless times to help companies with their numbers. You don't need a CPA to do this, just someone familiar with corporate finance.

4) Designer / Creative

No matter how good your idea is you need someone to make it look presentable. Whether it's prototype, website, pitch deck, packaging or product design you need a designer to make it look attractive to customers, as well as investors. This person should also have general social media and online marketing knowledge.

5) Engineer

There are several types of engineers, and they all do very different things. If your venture has a software component you'll probably want a programmer or software engineer.

These people might be familiar with a number of development languages but not others, so make sure they can do what you need them to do. If you're a hardware company you may also need an electrical engineer, industrial engineer and/or mechanical engineer.

6) Operations
This role is very important, especially if you have a physical location or have a complex strategy. Typically this isn't something you'll need right off the bat, but you will need this for long term success.

So, you ask, where do I find people like this? It may surprise you that I am not a fan of 90 percent of networking events. If they cost a lot to go to, they are usually a waste of time, money and business cards. The first one I ever went to was at the Microsoft campus in the San Francisco Bay Area and they claimed to have a 3-to-1 start-up to investor ratio. I spent $250 to get in and didn't meet one actual investor. I went to several more to be sure and, yup, same result. The people who do go to these events are service providers like bookkeepers, lawyers, fractional CFO services, designers, marketing people and anyone who wants to sell things to start-ups. By going to these events the service providers assume three things about you: You don't know what you're doing, you're super early and you have some money to spend.

That being said, there are other events that provide excellent opportunities. You can often find free events to go to, like meet-up events or 1MC (One Million Cups), where you can meet some great start-up folks. The trick is to find events in your market that are run by someone who is genuinely there to help start-ups and not to just make money off of them.

When I moved from the Bay Area to Boulder, Colorado, I didn't know anyone, and it was during this time that I was in the midst of building my BaziFIT team. To build my team, I just spoke to as many people as I could. I'd go to breweries, bars and coffee shops and speak to everyone who would talk to me. I'd ask what they do and find out what skills they have, and if I needed that skill I'd get their info and start engaging with them. Often, people involved in start-ups know others also involved in start-ups, so once you get to know one you can usually get introductions to others.

I met both my product manager and my algorithmic genius at bars, and from there they introduced me to both their circles and I was able to build my team. If someone has skills, fits the company culture and is willing to work for equity, I'm willing to give them a shot. If I had to choose between two candidates for a position at my company, where one is extremely good at what I'm looking for but doesn't jive in the culture of the company and the other jives with the culture but might be a little less polished, I'm going for the culture fit every time.

If you're a developer, hackathons are a great way to meet potential team members. They are events where over a day or weekend groups of developers and entrepreneurs try to solve a problem or come up with a start-up idea. I'm familiar with a couple of companies born from hackathons.

If you need a team member with a business specialty, go to your local University with an MBA program (or program of desired specialty) and ask them if they can recommend any students. My MBA program required an unpaid internship and I was lucky enough to be able to fine-tune my finance skills at my uncle's oil company.

So now that you know who you need, how are you going to compensate them?

If you have raised funds or have your own individual resources you'll have to decide how best to spread your resources. So, let's take a look at how this works. If you're familiar with Karl Marx you'll know that any output is equal to capital + labor. But what does this mean? Let's take a deeper dive.

How are there two inputs when a company starts off with only one thing—equity? Because a company sells equity for capital. However, there is another way. Instead of selling the equity for cash once, you can get people to work for you in exchange for equity. There are some tricks to this, you can't just give people equity and expect them to continue doing their job. That is why typical equity compensation agreements have a vesting agreement that covers the terms of the engagement. I believe it is better to give the equity to my team rather than to investors, thus making sure the labor part of the equation receives the majority of the benefits of success.

There are two components to the typical vesting agreement. The first component is "vesting terms" which cover the amount of equity the person is receiving and the time period that the equity is given to the person. For example Person X is receiving 240,000 shares distributed monthly spread out over two years, so every month Person X is receives 10,000 shares. The second component is "the cliff" which is the minimum amount of time Person X needs to stay with the company before being able to keep any equity. For example, if Person X had a one year cliff, and Person X leaves after 11 months, instead of leaving with 110,000 shares they would walk away with nothing.

I knew a CEO who would hire people who didn't seem to last more than a year. One day I spoke to one of his new employees and they mentioned that they had a 12 month cliff and were being paid 90 percent in equity. The CEO was hiring people then firing them right before their cliff expired. This is highly unethical.

Here's another example. Let's say you have an app or web platform that you want to develop. Now let's also assume you are a capable designer and developer. What do you need to make the platform? Because you're a developer, the only thing required to actually create your platform is your own labor. So with no need to raise funds, you can simply make the product and test the market for product/market fit. Meaning that in your equation there is no need for capital, only labor.

Now how about if you're a designer and don't know how to program. In this case you can design the platform but unless you pay someone to develop it you won't have a finished product. So you find an investor who likes your vision and you convince them to give you the funds to pay a developer who will turn your design into a working platform.

Before the investor gives you money, you and the investor need to agree on a valuation that compensates them for their funds and the risk they are taking.

In summary:

- It is critical to build a team with the skills you will need to either be successful or take you to your next set of milestones.
- Each business has different needs based on the skills of the team and the goals you have for your business.
- It is a strategic choice to either give equity to your team or raise funds and pay the team in cash.

The *real* Art of the Deal...

A lot of people think finance is difficult so they try to avoid it. I ask that you give it a shot because it is very important for entrepreneurs to know the basics of finance. Because I'm trying to be brief, this is going to get a little dense. I'm going to try to break this down into layman's terms. If you really want to understand this material I highly recommend reading more about it. I understand getting an MBA or a Masters in Finance or Entrepreneurship isn't feasible for most people, but you can audit classes at your local program.

Before I start I want to direct your attention to an important issue that I've seen many founders without a business background run into. If you are going to compensate people via equity, it is important to give out equity **PRIOR** to raising a large amount of funds. Before raising funds, the value of your shares are "nothing" because there is no previous sale price to peg the value. Thus, when you issue people shares as compensation they are not receiving anything of value. The receiver of the shares doesn't need to pay tax on the value of the shares because there is no value to tax.

If you raise funds prior to working out your equity compensation and the shares are $1 per share, and you give someone 10,000 shares as compensation for work, that person has to pay income tax on those shares because they are being issued for compensation. The IRS just sees that the individual had an extra income of $10,000 real dollars and not $10,000 worth of shares.

This is one reason why options are given. If I give a new team member options to buy 10,000 shares at a 20-50% discount, the only actual compensation is whatever you're paying the person. These shares are taken from your option pool, that you create when setting up your capitalization table, or cap table. The other thing you'll need to account for in the cap table is the equity you'll be giving investors for your first round.

Let's talk about Rounds of Investment. Your first round is a "seed" round because it is meant to turn your idea into a prototype or functioning product. Seed rounds are typically from friends, family members, founders or angel investors. The next rounds will be categorized starting from series A and progressing down the alphabet. Series A rounds are typically from venture capital, family offices and angels, and meant to scale your product or service into a revenue generating company.

If you have an investor and you're trying to figure out what to give them in exchange for their hard earned cash, there are essentially three options: debt, convertible debt and equity.

- **Debt** is what it sounds like, the investor gives you money and you give them a note guaranteeing repayment with interest.

- **Convertible debt** is debt that can be converted to equity depending on the terms. The debt either remains debt until the investor or company elect to convert it into equity, or an event occurs that converts the debt into equity. You can get creative and set the conversion trigger to be whatever you want.

- **Equity** is shares in your company. There are two main types of equity: common shares and preferred shares. There are also exotic types of shares that I will cover later, but for this example I'll keep it simple. Common shares are what founders retain. They typically have one vote and are subordinate to preferred shares and debt in terms of payback upon dividend issuance or liquidation of the company. Preferred shares are typically held by investors because they have priority over common on payback, but are subordinate to debt holders. However, preferred shares typically don't have as much voting power as common shares.

Now, let's cover some of the exotic equity types. One cool thing about having your own business is that you have the flexibility to do whatever you want in terms of equity; seriously, almost anything.

Example 1: Golden Shares—shares that have a very large amount of votes and can eclipse a majority of outstanding shares, allowing founders to retain voting control while not numerically being the majority owner. Mark Zuckerberg did this with Facebook.

Example 2: Phantom Shares—shares used to compensate team members. The advantage is that these shares don't actually exist until a liquidation event, which means that you don't need to pay taxes on your equity.

Here is an example of a simple single class capitalization (cap) table. In this example you have raised $1,000,000 from three angel investors. They take a combined 50% ownership of your company. The other 50% is spread out amongst the team for their sweat equity (unpaid work that they performed to earn shares of the company). Because no one person has a majority you can still lead if you are a consensus builder. You should always maintain good relationships with your shareholders. This is especially important when you don't own a majority of the votes.

If you are concerned about equity then you can raise less funds or increase your evaluation. If you can't do either of those things then you can play with the amount of classes of shares your company has and the votes associated with each class.

Shareholder	Seed Investment	Sweat Equity	Shares	Ownership Stake
Tom	$ 300,000	$ 0	300,000	15.00%
Jane (CEO)	$ 0	$ 400,000	400,000	20.00%
Ashley (CTO)	$ 0	$ 300,000	300,000	15.00%
Jose	$ 300,000	$ 0	300,000	15.00%
Hamid	$ 400,000	$ 0	400,000	20.00%
Ali (Designer)	$ 0	$ 200,000	200,000	10.00%
Option Pool	$ 0	$ 0	100,000	5.00%
Funds Raised	$ 1,000,000			
Total Shares			2,000,000	100%
Price Per Share	$ 1			

Below is an example of a more complex cap table. In this example your venture will have two classes of shares. Class A shares have ten times the number of votes as Class B shares. This means if you give Class A to your founders and Class B to your investors, the founders will keep control of major decisions.

Typically, you can only ask for shares with ten times the voting power if you have a company that has a high interest from investors. If you're desperate for funds, you will probably not be able to pull off this.

Shareholder	Investment	Class A (10X Vote)	Class B	Stake	Votes
Tom	$ 300,000	0	300,000	15.0%	3.0%
Jane (CEO)	$ 0	400,000	0	20.0%	39.6%
Ashley (CTO)	$ 0	300,000	0	15.0%	29.7%
Jose	$ 300,000	0	300,000	15.0%	3.0%
Hamid	$ 400,000	0	400,000	20.0%	4.0%
Ali (Designer)	$ 0	150,000	0	7.5%	14.9%
Option Pool	$ 0	50,000	100,000	7.5%	5.9%
Funds Raised	$ 1,000,000			100.0%	100.0%
Total Shares		900,000	1,100,000	2,000,000	10,100,000
Price Per Share	$ 1.00				

Next, you will need to determine the valuation of your shares. Valuation is always a difficult decision for start-ups. You will need to consider many things, including the team, intellectual property, assets, brand recognition, first mover advantage, etc. However, at the end of the day it comes down to what the investor is willing to pay and what you as a founder are willing to give up. Below, I'm going to cover some of my favorite valuation methodologies starting with the easiest.

If your company is early stage or pre-revenue then you'll want to use one of these next two valuation methods. This chapter increases in complexity as you go, so if you feel lost you can skip ahead to the next chapter. If you're just starting off, then I suggest you at least get past the cash flow section.

If your company is generating revenue then you can explore one of the more complicated discounted cash flow methods. If you try to use a cash flow based method before you have cash flows you will encounter pushback on your projections, so make sure they are conservative (a.k.a. they don't look like a hockey stick) and defensible (a.k.a. you have clear and plausible assumptions).

Comparable: This is the simplest way to value a company. Look for companies in a similar space and stage that have raised funds, then use their valuation to justify yours. I typically use crunchbase.com to find this information.

Replacement value: The next easiest method is to figure out the value of each member of the team and the progress you've made. This method is typically used if there are no barriers to entry (such as patents, first mover advantage or strategic partners) for competitors. The table below shows an example of these values charted.

Value Add	Value
Team	$ 500,000
IP	$ 500,000
Prototype	$ 100,000
Assets	$ 30,000
Total	$ 1,130,000

Advanced Valuation techniques, for companies that have cash flow. But what are cash flows?

Let's think about all the money going into and out of a company. You have revenues, then you subtract operating expenditure and capital expenditures and you have profits. Subtract taxes and you have net or post-tax profits. Some companies reinvest so much of their revenues into capital expenditures that they have no profit, thus pay no tax.

Because profits aren't a good indicator of a company's health, many people look at **EBITDA** (Earnings Before Interest Taxation Depreciation and Amortization) instead. Basically, after revenues you subtract cost of goods sold and operating expenditures but don't take out capital expenditures.

For those who are unfamiliar with capital expenditures and operating expenditures, I'll briefly explain these concepts and their differences.

A **capital expenditure** is a cost incurred by a business that leads to an asset or something that can be depreciated. Examples include: machinery, computers, buying office equipment, land and inventory.

An **operating expenditure** is a cost incurred by a business that is related to non-asset expenses such as: rent, leased office equipment, salaries and utilities.

The first step is to construct a "base case" scenario that is the combination of the most reasonable key assumptions for future cash flow. These include the following basic assumptions:

- Activity timelines: start-up period, build period, maturity period (3-20 years total depending if you plan to sell or continue operating the venture)
- Unit sales volumes
- Raw materials and finished product inventory
- Corporate overhead
- Marketing and advertising expense
- Transportation costs
- Sales price
- Capital expenditures
- Income and other taxes
- Working capital requirements
- Unit cost of goods sold

In addition to raw materials and other direct inputs, the cost of goods sold contains both fixed and variable operating costs.

Fixed costs generally do not change with sales volume, while variable costs are directly connected to the level of sales.

The more detailed the breakdown of your assumptions, the more reliable your future projection. It is essential to not use the WAG technique, which is defined as "wild ass guesses!" All assumptions should be documented for their basis in order that an investor may verify them during their due diligence.

The cash flow profile you have created is also a useful budget to present to investors. This dual purpose will save you time and effort. You can have more than one scenario besides the "base" case, such as an "upside" case and a "minimum" case. Try not to have more than three cases, though, or you will overwhelm a potential investor with "**analysis paralysis**."

Let's quickly go over what your cash flows should look like. Say you're a company generating revenue and you have operating expenditures and capital expenditures. This is a very basic example your cash flows:

Item	2019	2020	2021
Revenues	$ 1,000,000	$ 4,500,000	$ 10,000,000
Operating Expenditures			
Salaries	$ 500,000	$ 900,000	$ 2,000,000
Rent and Utilities	$ 100,000	$ 175,000	$ 400,000
Services	$ 250,000	$ 425,000	$ 1,000,000
Capital Expenditures			
Facility	$ 500,000	$ 0	$ 0
Equipment	$ 250,000	$ 250,000	$ 500,000
Facility Improvement	$ 0	$ 200,000	$ 1,000,000
EBITDA	$ 150,000	$ 3,000,000	$ 6,600,000
Profit	$ (600,000)	$ 2,550,000	$ 5,100,000
Yearly NPV 25%	$ 120,000	$ 1,920,000	$ 3,379,200
Valuation	$ 5,419,200		

Net Present Value (NPV): In this calculation you need to put together a projection of cash flows.
The formula is:

$$\frac{\text{future cash flow or EBITDA}}{(1 + \text{interest rate})^{\text{time}}}$$

The interest rate is calculated by finding out what the capital could have done elsewhere. I typically use 25% because of the risk.

Risk Adjusted NPV: After you have the cash flows, instead of using the simple 25% discount rate, you can use real world risks that could prevent you from getting to your ideal scenario ignorer to discount the cash flows more accurately.

You come up with the likelihood, as a percentage, a risk will cause a failure in the venture. You then multiply the percentages against each other. Using that result you subtract that from one and multiply that number by the unadjusted value.

Risk Item	Probability
Team execution	90%
Product/market fit	80%
Contractor execution	95%
Patent	75%
Risk Adjustment	**51.30%**

Or perhaps your venture is high risk and high reward, thus your discount should be much higher. Imagine a venture where you have less than a 10% chance of success, but if you do succeed it will be worth $100 million dollars!

Risk Item	Probability
Successful prototype	50%
Successful demonstration product/service	50%
Achieving the target sales rollout	50%
Probability of achieving the target sales maturity	50%
Overall probability of success	**6.25%**

Therefore, if you calculated a USD $100 million NPV at 10% discounted cash flow the risk net present value would be USD $6.25 million. If you valued your company at USD $10 million in other ways, you would require a 10% probability of success to achieve this value.

At the end of the day, the valuation of your company is whatever the investor(s) and you, the founder, agree upon. It is important that everyone is properly compensated for risks and efforts. The above methods are just a starting point for negotiations. Most seed or series A deals end up with investors taking 10-25% of the company.

In summary, there are several ways to structure a deal and several methods to value a company. Your end goal should be to structure a deal that works well for both parties and compensates everyone fairly. It is critical to adequately incentivize the team, compensate investors' risk, and bring in enough money / resources to take the company to the next set of milestones.

Marketing

When most people think about marketing they think advertising. That is just a very small part of what marketing is. Marketing is everything that has to do with your product or customers. It covers obvious things like websites, social media pages and advertising; but it also includes less obvious things like product design, pricing and product features. It is my intent to explain the components of marketing that impact a start-up the most.

Product

Is your product a physical product that needs to be designed and manufactured like a Tesla vehicle? Is it an app that needs to be built like Facebook? Is it SaaS (software as a service) like Spotify? Is the product or service B2B (business to business) like Intel or B2C (business to consumer) like Apple? Do you require a brick and mortar storefront like Walmart? Or can the product be sold through an online retailer like Amazon?

Pricing

There are three areas of pricing that are of importance: price elasticity, contribution margin and price discrimination.

Depending on the price elasticity of demand, your product will be either elastic or inelastic. If your product is **elastic** then there is a strong relationship between price and demand, meaning that your consumers are highly price sensitive. If you lower the price you sell more and if you raise the price your sales vanish.

A good example of this is airline travel for vacationers. If prices drop, more people fly to destinations for vacation rather than driving or taking a staycation. Conversely, If airline prices rise then people who were going to fly for leisure or convenience would consider driving or just staying at home.

This relationship is completely different for business travelers, which is conversely an **inelastic** market. A business traveler would have to pay significantly more to deter them from flying. As long as the trip doesn't suck the margin out of the deal, a businessman will travel. There is, of course, a point where the price of flying becomes so high that substitutes come into play, such as video conferencing.

Contribution margin, simply stated, is so you can understand if you're making enough money per sale. It is the difference between production cost and sale price divided by the sale price, giving you the portion of sales price that is your "profit." So If I'm selling a product for $50 and it costs me $20 to produce, there's a contribution margin of 60%. Typically you want your contribution margin to be at least 45%. If you have a business with high fixed costs or overhead you may need a higher contribution margin to make sure your business is profitable. The calculation looks like:

Sale Price ($50) - Production Cost ($20) = 60% margin
Sale Price ($50)

A simple example of price discrimination is the movie industry. In this example let's say there is an exciting new blockbuster coming out. People who really, really want to see the movie will spend $20 to see it in 3D in a high tech theater with reclining seats because, to them, seeing the movie this away has high intrinsic value. People who don't necessarily need all the bells and whistles will see it in a less expensive theater, spending $10. Another group may wait for the movie to be made available to rent, spending only $5 on the movie. Finally, some will simply wait for the movie to come out on TV or their streaming service and not spend anything other than their normal monthly subscription price to HBO or Netflix on the movie. At the end of the day, everyone saw the same movie but paid entirely different amounts.

- **Product Market Fit**

The most critically important part of marketing is to ensure that you're selling the right product to the right group of people. You could have the perfect product, but if you aren't targeting the right group of people you won't be successful.

You may feel that you have a product that can fit into multiple market segments, but there is always one market segment that is either going to be easier to enter or more profitable.

Imagine if you had an AI predictive analytics start-up. You have the rare opportunity to be able to enter almost any market, because every business can benefit from advanced models to gain more accurate predictions.

Some markets can be identified as "low-hanging fruit" (a phrase used to identify the easiest opportunities to reach). These include individual investors, financial services, private equity, public banking, consumer product companies and governments.

All of the aforementioned industries can benefit from AI services, but the real question is, what industry would be the easiest to enter, as well as the most profitable?

There isn't a "right" answer, because so much of success has to do with execution, however, it is critical to use your best reasoning, or game theory, to determine the market you are going to tackle first.

Knowing your customer and why they are buying your product is key. I recommend spending time talking to customers and potential customers to truly understand what value you are providing.

Go-To-Market

Once you have figured out your product, price and market fit, you now have to come up with a plan to take your product to market. Go-to-market can vary greatly depending on the industry.

Some industries have dedicated go-to-markets. For instance, in some states, if you brew beer you can only distribute your beer through a licensed beer distribution company; it is actually illegal to sell your beer directly to liquor stores.

Some industries are more traditionalist in nature and use methods that are familiar to the stakeholders. In those markets, if you go outside the norm, you'll often be fighting an uphill battle.

The medical industry is like that. If you have a medical device, good luck taking the product directly to medical provider's offices or clinics. Medical devices are typically distributed via distribution companies that have relationships with providers in geographic areas. They make these relationships by wining and dining the healthcare providers. Because the healthcare market in the U.S. is so fragmented, with many providers having their own offices and few large companies or networks, it is very expensive to reach all of the decision makers at each medical practice. That is why medical distribution is so difficult to do as a start-up.

Sometimes a company can find an innovative way to disrupt this incumbent method of distribution. Amazon did this perfectly in the book industry - I'd be willing to bet you didn't get this book from Barnes and Noble.

One thing you don't want to do is say: Market X is worth $50 billion, and we are going after 1% of that market, meaning we are going to make $500 million in revenue. This is the absolute biggest rookie mistake. What you need to do is identify an actual plan to gain market share. How will you get your first customer, and then 10 customers, and then how will you scale to hundreds and thousands? Do not oversimplify this, as investors are very serous about seeing a realistic plan. A good book about this is Zero to One by Peter Thiel.

Online Presence

Every business (even stealth start-ups) need a web presence. Your online strategy will differ depending on your business. It is important to have a good designer and developer to maximize your potential.

Social Media

The keys to a good social strategy will include: posting regularly, posting engaging high quality content, using hashtags like salt (you need some for flavor but too much will ruin the dish) and most importantly, keeping it professional.

Website

The first thing on your website should be a call to action. E-mail collection should be one of the first things people see when landing on your page. Having a clear, singular call to action is critical when you're trying to convert web traffic into customers. DailyBurn.com is a great example. They push their 30 day free trial relentlessly; there is little more you can do on their site other than sign up for the free trial.

Next, you want to ensure your website is search engine optimized (SEO). Make sure all the meta-tags are correctly set up, make sure your website text reiterates key words you think people will search and make sure your images are correctly named. Make a list of key words or phrases that you feel people may search for when looking for your product, then use these words as often as you can in your website.

Graphics are key, most people don't want to read paragraph after paragraph of straight text. Say what you want in one or two sentences as often as possible. If you want some guidance, look at Apple's website as the gold standard. They are always on the forefront of design.

Name / Logo

A good name is brief, memorable, easy to spell and doesn't translate negatively in other languages. A cool recent trend is to incorporate your web address suffix in your name, like <u>ouo.io</u>. I recommend coming up with four or five top contenders for names and do a survey or focus group to help pick your name.

Your logo generally takes more time to develop than the name. Once you have your name, use it as inspiration to come up with the logo. Depending on your industry, you may want to pick certain colors or a design strategy that will be familiar to the market. This is where an experienced designer becomes very helpful.

Market Research

There are two types of market research, secondary and primary. **Secondary market research** is the aggregation of statistics and articles, as well as other research you have found that was done by others, but is still applicable to your company. This is often the first step because it is infinitely easer than conducting your own research. **Primary market research** is done within the company and includes surveys, focus groups and competitive analysis.

Surveys should be between 5 and 20 questions, and should not take more than 10 or 15 minutes to complete. Anything longer and you'll need to pay the participants or find another way to incentivize them.

Start off with demographic and other segmentation questions such as gender, income, education, age or Android vs. iOS preference. Make sure you don't bias the survey taker by telling them about your company until you are on the last few questions, if at all.

You want to ask straightforward questions, and avoid "double-barreled questions" that attempt to cram two or more questions into one. An example of this is: "Do you like hot coffee from Starbucks?" This question should be broken down into 3 questions: "Do you like coffee?", "Do you prefer hot coffee?" and "From 1 to 4 with one being dislike and 4 being love, where would you rank Starbucks coffee?"

The types of responses you want are the following. Straight forward True / False or Yes / No, ranking options (consider if you want an odd or even number of options, you may want an odd if you're OK with people picking the middle option or even number if you prefer them not pick a middle option), multiple choice (typically not giving more than 4 or 5 options), word association, and long-form answers (you typically only want to use one of these, and keep in mind this is only to add context, you won't be able to easily tabulate the results). When tabulating you want to see how people answer questions in relation to other questions. For example: Do people who like hot coffee prefer Starbucks more than those who like cold coffee?

Focus groups should be between 5 and 9 people and last about 30 to 90 minutes. You want enough people so that the discussion isn't dominated by one person, yet you want a small enough group where everyone gets a chance to give their opinion. It is typical to compensate participants. Make sure you go into the focus group with a plan and key points you want discussed.

To run a focus group successfully there should be a team guiding and overseeing the focus group. There should be a moderator to make sure no one person dominates the discussion and that everyone is participating. He or she would, when necessary, ask direct questions, but generally just guide the conversation to cover all necessary objectives of the focus group. There should also be one or two people taking notes on the responses from the participants. Ideally, they are behind one-way glass so the participants can't see what the notetakers are reacting to. If this is not feasible be sure to avoid biasing the participants through body language or other means. The focus group should be recorded so the team can review the footage later to see if they missed anything.

In terms of competitive analysis the two most common are SWOT and Porter's 5 Forces.

The **SWOT analysis** is used to identify Strengths, Weaknesses, Opportunities and Threats to your business. The first two are focused on internal elements: strengths and weaknesses that are specific to your company. The second two are focused on external elements: opportunities and threats to your industry.

Strengths (Internal, impacts your company)	Weaknesses (Internal, impacts your company)
• Do you have a strong team? • Do you have a functioning prototype? • Beta testers? • Applied for provisional patents?	• Need business development team? • Need funds? • Need a prototype?
Opportunities (External, impacts whole industry)	Threats (External, impacts whole industry)
• Is the industry projected to grow at an annual rate of 25% by 2030? • No market dominating firm? • Low customer acquisition costs?	• Low level of customer loyalty? • Large number of new market entries? • Potential government regulation?

Porter's 5 Forces was developed by Michael Porter, a well-known Harvard Business School professor. He suggested breaking the analysis of your market down into five areas: Threat of New Entries, Power of Buyers, Power of Suppliers, Threat of Substitutes and Competitive Rivalry. You basically give the importance of each element (strong, moderate, weak) and discuss the market element.

Threat of New Entries: Strong

- Often it is easy for a company to enter a market
- Unless it is a heavily regulated market
- Or has high costs and low margins, reducing the likelihood of new investment in the space

Power of Buyers: Strong

- Typically customers have the control to switch
- Unless you have a monopoly or have high switching costs

Power of Suppliers: Moderate

- Typically it is pretty easy to switch manufacturing firms
- Unless you have high switching costs, or are licensing a technology or trademark
- If you're a software service, then how hard is it to find developers who can do what you need?

Threat of Substitutes: Strong

- If a customer can receive the same or similar benefit from somewhere else
- Have a wide definition of substitute

Competitive Rivalry: Moderate

- Do companies in the space go after each other like beer or car industries?
- Or is the market more calm like local competition between bars and gasoline stations?
- Is the market saturated or underserved, consolidated or fragmented?

In summary:

- Marketing is more than just advertising.

- Product/market fit is paramount.

- A strategy for going to market by targeting your market niche is critical.

Your First Investor

Finding investors is the hardest part for most entrepreneurs. I say most because some people already have connections to capital, making fundraising much easier or even unnecessary. There are also some ventures that don't require a large initial investment, and if that is your case then you are indeed lucky. For the rest of us, here are my thoughts.

Nepotism is rife in the funding arena. It is almost impossible to raise initial funds from someone you cold call; it happens, but don't bet on it. The cold hard truth is that most successful start-ups receive between $500,000 to $1 million as seed financing (this is the name of the round that brings the venture off of the napkin and into reality). Because seed rounds are typically done well before a prototype or MVP (minimally viable product), it is typically raised from friends and family.

The glaring issue here is that if you don't come from money and don't have a rich uncle you are likely to have difficulty pulling together the amount of money you will need to effectively get your idea off the ground. This is the unspoken truth of entrepreneurship: It's a game for the rich. This is something that deeply troubles me and is at the heart of why I believe in a universal basic income scheme, which would empower people who wish to become entrepreneurs but lack the financial resources.

My family isn't trust fund-rich, but in my journey in entrepreneurship I've had hundreds of thousands of dollars worth of help from them. This money has paid for my rent and living expenses for over a decade. Sure, it can be seen as an investment in me by my parents, and I'm sure any parent would want to do this for their child, but this isn't financially feasible for a vast majority of people. If I had to work a 40 to 60 hour per week job to make ends meet, I wouldn't have the time or energy to work on my projects.

There are plenty of side gigs to make money when your venture doesn't have enough money to pay you. I've coached soccer, taught part-time at a business school, done handyman work, business consulting and even started an Etsy shop with my wife. If you have skills that can directly lead to cash, it is a massive advantage when starting a business.

I knew someone who had a start-up in the Bay Area. During a seven year period, despite their product becoming obsolete, they were able to raise more than $50 million, continually raising funds throughout the time period simply with their connections and hanging out at swanky San Francisco bars.

This is why networking is so important. I can't be more brutally honest, to start a company you need a rich ally. It is sad but true, when you're in undergrad or grad school try and find people with money. When you're out and about, try and network with people who have money. When you're fundraising, go to a nice bar and network with people who have money. These connections will be critical to getting those seed funds. But I want to make it clear that I'm not encouraging anyone to be fake or manipulative. And you shouldn't be friends with someone just because they have money. I've cut plenty of wealthy people out of my life because they were toxic; money definitely isn't everything. Nevertheless, the old saying, "It's not what you know, but who you know," does ring true in this instance.

The only way entrepreneurship can be a legitimate option for the majority of Americans is if we somehow either make seed financing more readily available or alleviate the financial pressure of entrepreneurs through a universal basic income type system.

Once you've found your investor, you need to figure out how much you need to raise and when. This is critically important; if you don't raise enough money to get to your next milestone your venture will be stuck in the mud, unable to move forward. The trick is to write down all the milestones required to get to your end goal, then group those milestones into chunks or tranches. Figure out the cost of completing the first group of milestones and add 20%; things always take longer and are more expensive than expected. The main goal of the first chunk should be to build a testable prototype. Then you can raise more funds to refine the product and take it to market.

A bit of advice to take along with you is to hire a designer with relevant experience, especially UI (user interface) and UX (user experience). I've found that regardless of whether the app works, it needs to look presentable. A sleek app design that isn't working is basically equivalent to a working app prototype that looks like garbage.

For example, when we got our first BaziFIT prototype sensors / app combo, our app was as raw as it could be. It was basically a screen with a numerical value on it, because at the time we were more focused on the sensor data than the user experience. I realized my priorities were backward, and that investors would have preferred a pretty user interface even if it didn't work well.

In summary:

- If you have wealthy friends or family then don't be too proud to ask them for seed capital.
- Make sure you get enough money to get to at least a prototype or market traction.
- Produce high quality images or video of your vision for the company. This will dramatically help in bringing on early stage investors.

What Investors Want

I've literally spoke to hundreds of investors and have received more "No" responses than anything, but I have received some "yes" responses. This is an attempt to help you learn from both my failures and successes.

Product Market Fit

This essentially confirms that the product you are developing and the market segment you're targeting are a match. Often, you'll need to tweak the product or tweak the market segment before you get a perfect match. This is the first thing that you'll need to convince the investor to take an interest in your company.

Pitch Decks

This is the second most important element when raising funds, aside from your relationships with investors. There is no perfect formula for a pitch deck, so you need to find what works best for your venture. A pitch deck is a presentation you physically give in front of an investor or group of investors. It should be customized to your audience and the amount of time you have to present. The pitch deck should look like an Apple keynote: almost no text, great imagery and a conversational tone. If you haven't already, watch Steve Jobs's 2007 iPhone Keynote for a perfectly executed pitch.

You're also going to want to put together a send out deck. A send out deck is a pitch deck you send out via e-mail. You're not physically there to explain the slides to potential investors, so you'll need your icons, images, text and infographics to do the talking. You'll need this type of deck to get an opportunity to pitch in person. An ideal send out deck will have 8 to 12 slides.

Here is a guideline for a send out deck, include the slides that are most applicable to your business:

- The Title Slide says the name of the company, has a catchy phrase or statement about the company, the round you're raising (pre-seed, seed, series A, series B …), and the date. I use the season so I don't have to keep changing the month.

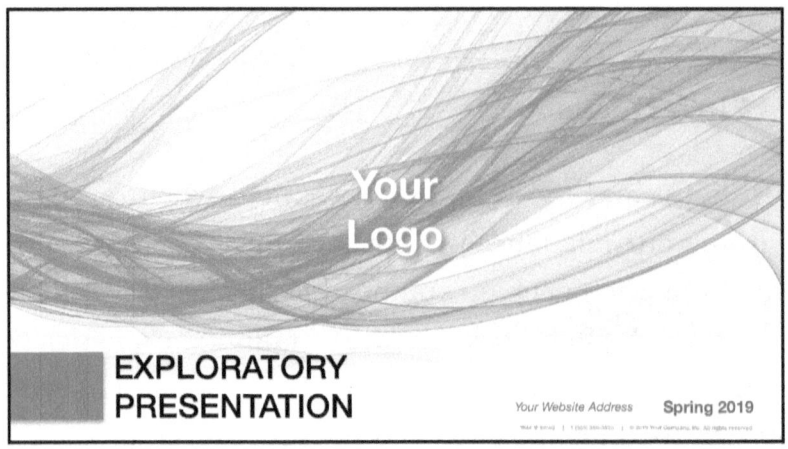

- To be safe it is good to include a disclaimer. The text should looks something like the following:

Corporate and other information provided herein contains forward-looking statements and pro-forma calculations. The reader is cautioned that the assumptions used in the preparation of such information and calculations, which are considered reasonable by _____, Inc. at the time of preparation, may prove to be incorrect. Actual results achieved during the forecast and prior periods will vary from the information provided herein and the variations may be material. There is no representation by _____, Inc. that actual results achieved during the forecast and prior periods will be the same in whole or in part as those projected. In addition, the technologies described herein are early stage and future results may differ materially from those anticipated.

- The Problem Slide is the first slide after the title and is the most important slide. This slide conveys the "why" to the reader. As in, why is this important? The why must be concise, and it must be heavy hitting. I would spend a good amount of time purely on this slide, as it is often the first slide you work on and the last one you finish.

You first want to cover what the problem is, and be sure to state it clearly and briefly. Then you go about showing why this problem is a big deal. Does it lead to deaths? Does it cost a lot because of inefficiencies it causes? Why don't current solutions work? Lastly, you never want to say that you have no competitors, it tells investors you are either naive or don't have an actual problem. If you don't have any direct competitors, talk about substitutes.

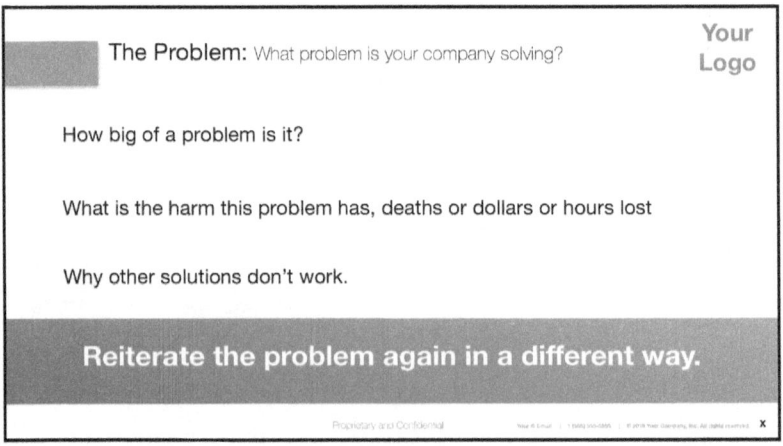

- The Solution Slide is the second most important slide. You need to parry the problem slide and land a harder counter punch solution (can you tell I was watching some boxing highlights on ESPN?). Try to use icons or imagery to show your solution.

Like the problem you want to be concise when unveiling your solution, less is always more. Images or icons are always helpful when describing something.

Always discuss benefits rather than features. Talk about the real reason someone is buying your product or service. Most of the time you can distill it down to either one or a few words.

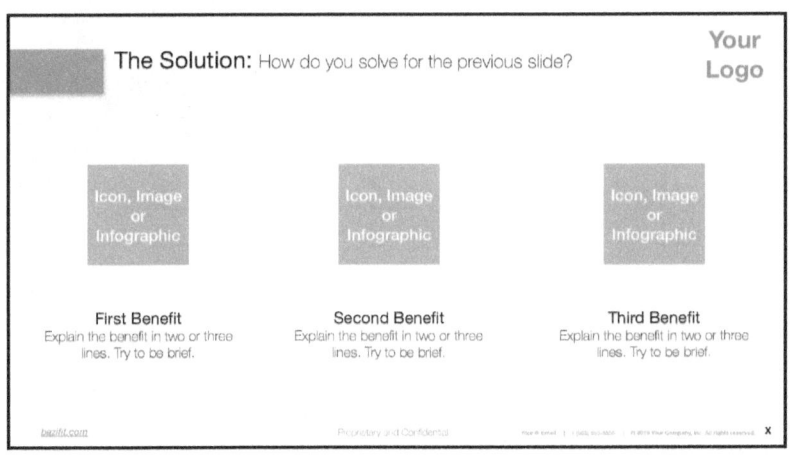

- If you have a new invention, you'll need to explain how it works. It is imperative that it is clearly stated, that's why I like a three step process. Each step should be clear and brief, no longer than five to seven words; just cover the big picture.

If you can show how all of the steps come together in an infographic that is always impactful. Sometimes a video works best, but try to keep any video content to under 30 seconds. Any longer and the viewers may become disengaged.

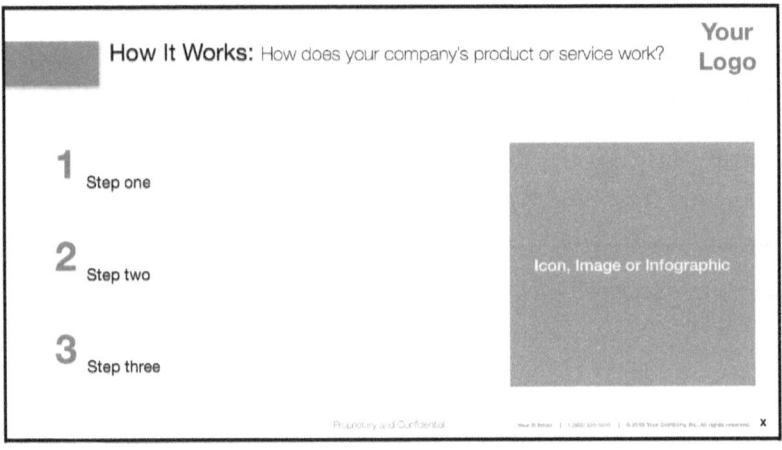

- The Market Size Slide is important to identify both your market validation and size. This shows investors that the pie you're after is big enough to satiate the investor's appetite for growth.

An effective way of doing this is showing stats on a company you'll be disrupting. They have X million paying customers and make $Y with Z% of the market. Make sure you site your sources and clearly indicate any assumptions you are making when you come up with your market size.

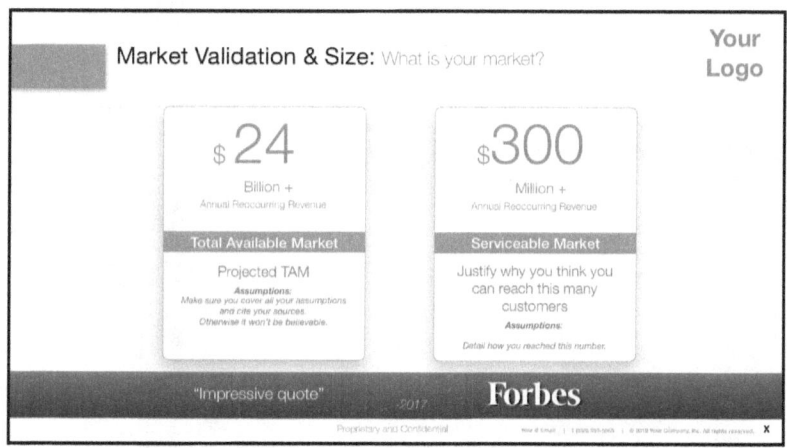

- Your Go-To-Market Strategy Slide is critical. If the investor doesn't believe that your plan to take your product to market is viable, it can stop the conversation dead in its tracks. You can have the best product in the world, but if you don't have a rollout plan you are going to struggle to find investors, thus limiting your success.

Cover your strategy in steps or phases while clearly delineating key objectives and actions that will lead to the completion of those objectives. As always, icons or an infographic would work well here. You don't need to talk numbers, just the overall game plan.

- A Team Slide is typically required unless you have a team that is too big, in which case you can just add a link to your website that lists the full team. I'd recommend not including more than 4 or 5 people on the slide. If you want to include more, break it up into two slides. For each team member, be sure to give a couple of reasons why they are important to the company.

- You'll want a Technical Slide showing how the product / technology works. Feel free to discuss anything non-confidential, but DO NOT DISCLOSE ANYTHING THAT YOU PLAN ON PATENTING. Intellectual property is important to talk about also, especially if you have issued patents. It is important not to disclose anything that could potentially be patented.

As I've said before, icons, infographics and video work great if you have them. Otherwise, sketches or renderings work well, too. If your company is an app, and you have wire frames or screen mockups, this is where you'd put them.

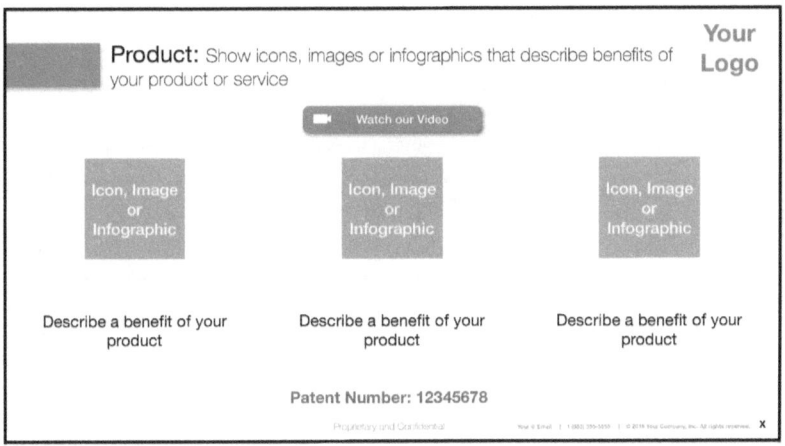

- Your Milestones / Timeline Slide is important to show investors where you see the company at the moment and where it's going in the short- and long-term.

If an investor is putting money into your company you need to sell them on what your plan is for their money. You can make quantifiable milestones such as sales numbers or a break even point, and/or general milestones such as entering new markets and improving the product.

Focus on the time immediately after you receive funding and where those funds will take your company. Regardless if you think your venture will be self-sufficient, you should still include your next round and even where a potential exit could occur.

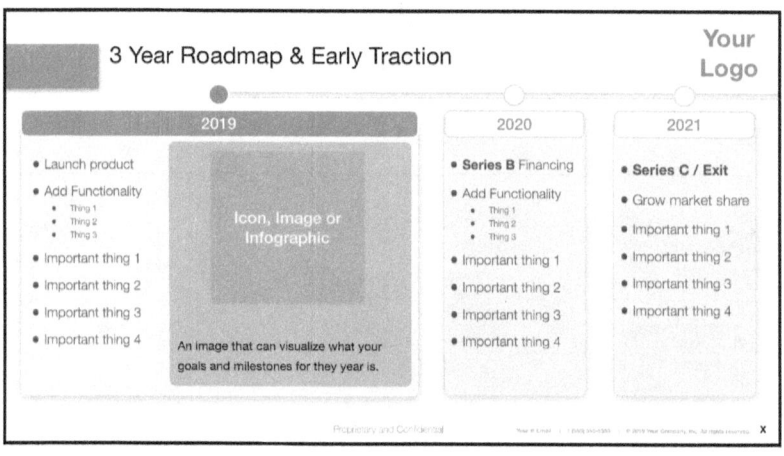

- Projections and assumptions are always incorrect, and investors know it. The point of making a Projections Slide is to show that you can put a believable model together.

It is critical to be transparent with your assumptions, and that your numbers add up. If an investor can't make the same logical steps needed to justify your numbers, they are far more unlikely to invest in your company.

This may require you to include more or different metrics than I include in this example. Whatever your key indicators are, I recommend including them in this slide.

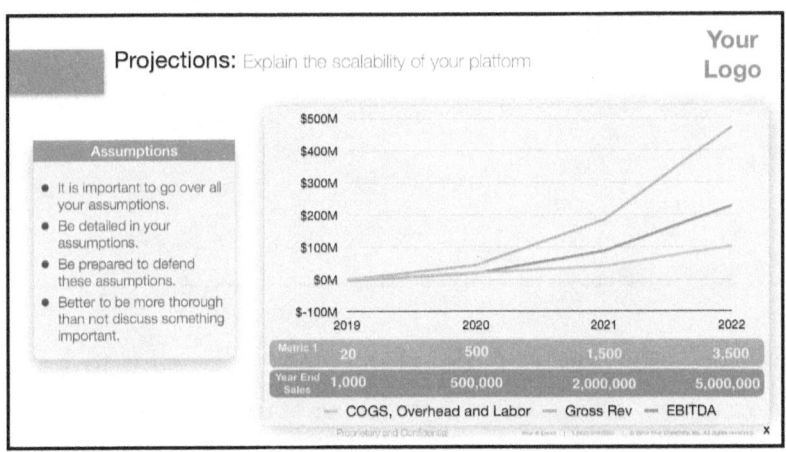

- A Competitor Analysis Slide is important for transparency and believability. If you say that you have no competitors then the investors will think either: a) There is no market there or b) There may be something there but you'll have to spend a ton of money to educate consumers.

I find Venn diagrams or a matrix with checkboxes both work well. You can use a classical quadrant diagram if you prefer, but they are often seen as cliche and aren't as easy to read.

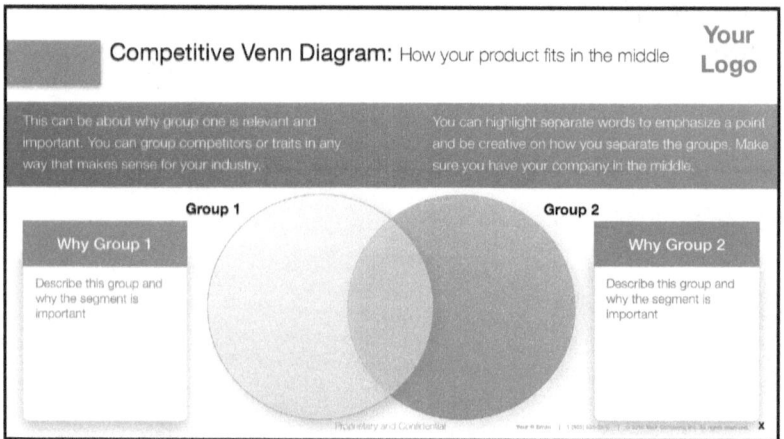

This may seem obvious but, for a Venn diagram to be useful you need to find two segments or groups that intersect. It could be based on product / service, high tech / low tech, high price / low price, millennials / baby boomers.

- Your Business Model and assumptions could take more than one slide. This is where you need to show why your approach will work and how it is superior to competitors. Identify how your business is different and if there is a competitive advantage your company has.

Are there market trends that would lead someone to believe that your venture is ahead of the curve or that this is the perfect time to invest in this market? Great, put that here.

Make sure you cite your sources, and if you're making extrapolations make sure you clearly indicate your assumptions. Whoever reads this slide may try to verify your claims.

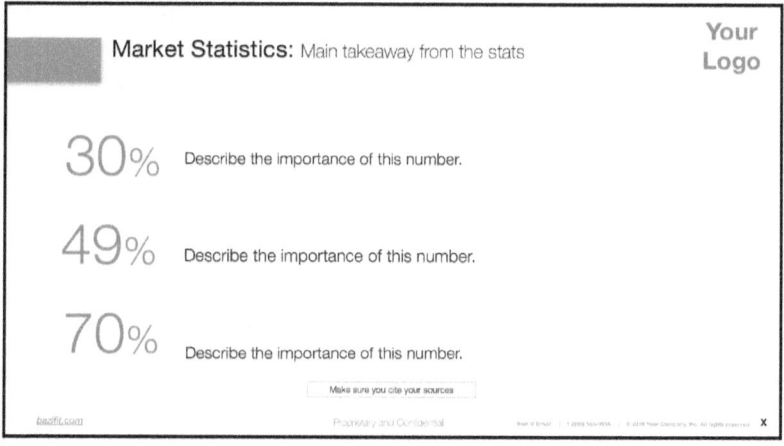

- An Ask Slide is required if you're sending the deck out to investors. However, and this is very important, if you are giving your pitch to non-accredited investors outside of friends and family, DO NOT INCLUDE THE ASK, IT IS ILLEGAL. This can be your last real slide, only followed by the "Thank You" slide, or you can discuss what you hope to achieve with those funds. I've seen both strategies successfully executed, it all depends on whether you want to leave them with your ask or your strategy.

Sometimes investors don't like to receive send out decks straight off of meeting you, in those cases they will ask you for an **Executive Summary**.

The document is between one and two pages and includes as many of the following items as possible. You may say, "How am I supposed to cover all these topics in under two pages?" I'd say "exactly." The purpose of the document is to show you can quickly and concisely convey the main essence of your company. Brevity is key!

- Overview of the company

<u>Company Name</u> is disrupting the <u>Blank Industry</u> by <u>doing this</u> and <u>that</u>. Similar to <u>industry leader</u> in that we <u>blank,</u> but unlike <u>industry leader</u> we <u>blank</u>.

Example 1: Uber is disrupting the transportation industry by democratizing the taxi industry by connecting a network of freelance drivers with people who need a ride. Similar to the conventional taxi system, but with fewer market inefficiencies.

Example 2: IKEA is disrupting the furniture industry by giving modern, price sensitive young adults the ability to access attractive home furnishings. Similar to other furniture stores, but less expensive, trendier and the user assembles the product themselves, making it easier to transport.

- What technology are you using with your venture and how are you creating and implementing it?

- What is the problem you are solving?

Focus on benefits not features. For example, instead of focusing on what you do, discuss the value you give your customers.

- Who are your competitors and what are your differences?

Venn diagrams, competitive matrixes and checklists are examples. Be sure to include substitutes, too, not just direct competitors.

- What is your market and what is its size?

TAM = Total Addressable Market. This can be: Number of Users, Annual Sales or Gross Total Sales. Depending on your industry and business you may choose any one or two of these metrics to show investors that this is a big, growing and attainable market. Don't show the entire market, come up with a reasonable amount of the market you think you can achieve. Be sure to have a plan detailing how you intend on getting there. Investors will surly press you on your assumptions.

You don't always want to show the biggest number. Say you're a smart watch start-up, you don't want to say, "our plan is to get .1% of the $3 trillion global consumer electronics industry." You want to say, "our plan is to get 10% of the $31 billion U.S. smart watch market." Both numbers are equal to $3 billion, but the latter example will get you a lot farther.

- What is your sales model to reach your market?

First, identify who your customers are: B2B (business to business), B2C (business to consumer), B2B2C (business to business to consumer), B2G (business to government).

Second, identify the method of reaching that audience. This is going to be dependent upon the market and your product. For example, if your company is an app, you may want to incorporate a referral program that gives current users a benefit when they refer a friend to the app. Or, if you're a health foods company, you may want to give out free samples.

- Do you have any traction to date?

This can be anything that shows that your business or product is desirable. It can be sales, pre-orders, mailing list sign-ups, social media followers or endorsement by key decision makers in the industry. That being said, the best metric is sales.

- Who is your competition?

It isn't just other companies in your industry, it can also be substitutes. For example, Coca Cola's biggest competitor is Pepsi, but Coke also competes with substitutes like milk, juice, sports drinks and water. A SWOT analysis and Porter's 5 Forces diagram are two great ways to analyze a competitive landscape. Other methods include mapping competitors on a two axis matrix looking at key indicators. Indicators that you can plot against each other include: price, quality, value to customer and level of technological advancement. Finally, you can always use a two or three circle Venn diagram.

- Who are the key people on the team?

Make sure you illustrate why the team you have can get the job done.

- Do you have any notable strategic partners or investors?

- Financials—how much can you make and what will be required to get to that point?

- What are your recent and next set of milestones?

Explain which milestones you have already reached, along with your next major events and how you're going to reach them. When fundraising, it is important to show what you've accomplished to date and what you want to accomplish with the investor's funds.

- Comparable section is to show investors the ask you have is comparable to other companies in your industry; www.crunchbase.com is a great resource for this.

Example Executive Summary:

Logo and Company Name

This executive business summary presents information concerning Company, Inc., a Colorado corporation, headquartered in Boulder, Colorado.

Overview   Company is a ___ that connects ___ and ___ with ___. Company's product is unique in its ability to _____, _____ and _____.

Technology   Company's patented (PN: 123456789) technology is hardware? software? What makes your tech unique?

Solutions   The Company's product is the basis for the following components:

    i. Something it does
    ii. Focus on Benefits
    iii. Not Features

[Infographic]

Competitive Differentiators

➤ Why are you different?
➤ Benefits of your uniqueness
➤ Why you're better

Market

7M	One part of your market
15M	Two parts of your market
<u>25M</u>	<u>Three parts of your market</u>
50M	Total potential customers with a total value of **$3B**

Sales Model   What is your go-to-market strategy? You should have a detailed plan. Make sure you elaborate on it and make sure it is believable.

[Infographic]

Validation   Any traction such as users or sales. What backs up your assertion that your company is a good idea? Cite sources.

Competition Current competitors include ___ out of ____, which offers _____ and _____, however it lacks _____. They are currently valued at $___.

The Team Our management team consists of **CEO** ____ - experienced entrepreneur, **COO** ____ - _____, **CTO** _____ - full stack developer, and **COO** _____ - _____. Our advisors include _____ - an experienced executive from the ____ space, _____ - an experienced tech executive and angel investor, and _____ - an experienced entrepreneur.

Investors To date, Company has raised more than $X00,000 from founders, friends, family, Angel Investors and the ____ Venture Accelerator. The funds were primarily used to _____, _____ and _____.

Projections

Assumptions
- It is important to go over all your assumptions.
- Be detailed in your assumptions.
- Be prepared to defend these assumptions.
- Better to be more thorough than not discuss something important.

	2019	2020	2021	2022
Metric 1	20	500	1,500	3,500
Year End Sales	1,000	500,000	2,000,000	5,000,000

— COGS, Overhead and Labor — Gross Rev — EBITDA

[cash-flow positive and break-even in ____]

Comparable Public companies in this market are trading at __x TTM sales. Private companies in the _____ space that have been recently acquired have been commanding __-__x revenues. (____ by ____ and _____ by _____)

Contact **Name**, Founder & CEO
555-555-5555 Name@company.com

There are many free resources online that can help you determine the types of documents you'll need when talking to serious investors about your company. One great free resource for corporate legal documents is www.cooleygo.com.

Articles of Incorporation

You can do this one yourself. Go to your Secretary of State website and see how to do it in your state. Many states, like Colorado, allow you to apply online. Lots of people think you need a Delaware entity to raise funds, but you can switch later on if you want to or if your investor requires you to do so. However, I'd recommend to doing it locally and saving money. Ideally you want to domicile your entity in a place that doesn't have a high yearly minimum tax, in case you are in development for several years before you start making revenue.

Corporate Bylaws

This document is like your company's constitution. Like the constitution outlines how the government works, your bylaws outline how your entity works. I recommend using generic ones, and not doing anything fancy.

Board Creation

Best to have a three-person board with an experienced Chairman.

Option pool and Outstanding Options

It is important to set aside enough equity to properly compensate and motivate your early employees. The pool you set aside now will need to cover all your new equity needs until you have another round of investments or a dilution event.

Cap Table

You'll want a detailed list of all of your investors and shareholders delineating the breakdown of all shares distributed. It is critical to keep this up to date. In addition to the cap table I'd recommend keeping a list of all investors with dates and amounts invested.

Projections

Using studied assumptions, try to build out your costs first then your future revenues. Make sure you project out three to five years of cash flows.

Valuation

Remember to indicate if you're referring to pre-money or post-money valuation. For example: $1 million for 20% equity would equate to a $5 million post-money valuation and a $4 million pre-money valuation. Don't be unrealistic; be modest with your valuations.

Tax ID / EIN

Once you incorporate your business in your state go to the IRS website and apply for an EIN. You will then indicate if you want to apply for an S-Corporation, which has some tax benefits.

Sales Tax License

When you're ready to start selling you'll need a sales tax license; apply for this at your state's Secretary of State website. If you're doing online sales you may also want to get a service like taxjar.com that can help you collect the right amount of taxes for each person.

Bank Account

Once you have your incorporation and EIN/Tax ID you can get a bank account. It will require signatures from shareholders so it will be easier to get your bank account prior to giving out shares.

In summary, every investor will want something different. You will need to have all your ducks in a row so that once the investor ask for a document you'll be able to send it over to them. It is important to look like you are prepared, and the best way to do that is to BE prepared. Part of being prepared is speaking with experts like attorneys and accountants that focus on startups. It's smart to have them review your documents and strategies.

Alternative Funding Sources

Interest in entrepreneurship has increased over the last couple of decades. This has lead to the creation of new ways for you to get resources for your business. I've explored these options and even tried a couple. I've also spoken with colleagues that have been successful using these avenues to be able to let you know what works.

Shark Tank

I can't even count how many people have suggested that I apply for Shark Tank. I actually have applied—three times. The first time I was way too early, the second time I went to a casting call and made it to the interview phase, the third time I sent in an e-mail and got through to the audition video phase, but they didn't like my video. I was told by the producers that I was too professorial and I that should focus on being more animated. I guess I wasn't over-the-top enough. I do know someone who actually made it onto the TV show. His product is in the wedding industry and he did his audition video in a wedding dress. Yes, you read that right, he did his pitch to get on Shark Tank while wearing a wedding dress. So if you are thinking about applying to Shark Tank, remember, their number one goal is to make entertaining reality TV, so don't focus overly hard on the numbers; focus on being entertaining.

Kickstarter / Indiegogo

I've done a very, very unsuccessful Kickstarter campaign. I don't think I even made it beyond 1% of my goal. However, I do know a team that raised more than $1 million on Kickstarter.

They spent three months collecting e-mail addresses and engaging their audience on social media. After they had enough people in their mailing list identify that they were ready to buy the product, they then launched the campaign and reached their goal in less than 24 hours.

They also spent more than $10,000 on an advertising / PR firm to help. The firm set up news interviews and had their story all over the news and social media. The team worked their butts off and executed perfectly, not to mention that their product was fully completed and ready to ship.

That was an example of a perfectly-timed campaign. If you try to run a campaign too early or without detailed planning then there is a far lower probability of success. The problem with getting too much attention before you have a prototype is that people get the feeling that they've seen your product and were unimpressed. It is much more difficult to get someone to change their initial impression compared with waiting and knocking their socks off when you're ready. Don't make your social media friends jaded by sharing too early; keeping people in suspense can be a good thing.

Incubators / Accelerators

Incubators and accelerators are great. They give start-ups resources to thrive and they also give credibility to a company. It's worth noting that not all accelerators are created equal. I've seen steep equity asked for with little offered in return. One accelerator asked for 8% for $20,000. That is a valuation of $250,000, which for most companies is an insult. In my experience, the best place to find accelerators is F6S.com.

Our team at BaziFIT attended an accelerator in an exclusive mountain town in Colorado. The accelerator asked for 3% for $30,000, so basically a $1 million valuation, which is a very good deal for an early-stage company.

Despite having an amazing time snowboarding and running into celebrities, I felt as though we were in a petting zoo. We had a lot of rich and successful mentors come in, but they didn't have time to learn anything about our businesses. They would come in and speak about themselves, we would ask 30 minutes of questions and they would be gone. So for future reference, if you apply to an accelerator, ask how engaged their mentors are, and don't get blinded by the glitzy list of Executives and VCs.

Unfortunately, the cost for three people to live there for five months ended up being more than the $5,000 we received for room and board, and because of the type of investors we met there, we didn't raise any funds from the network. Nevertheless, it was worth going because it added credibly to the company and the connections made there were invaluable.

Equity Crowdfunding

I have not used this method, mainly because it costs money to do the legal paperwork to offer shares to the general public. There are also plenty of scams in this arena, like firms promising investment if the start-up pays them several thousand dollars to do all the legal paperwork. As a general rule I have avoided this method. However, there do seem to be some legitimate equity platforms. I wouldn't pursue this method unless you need a large amount of money and you're doing something very philanthropic.

Grants

Grant are amazing if you have an academic background and experience applying for and receiving grants. If you don't have that experience it is very difficult and I suggest finding someone who does have that experience that can show you through the process. When I was considering applying for a grant through the NIH (National Institutes for Health) I called the NIH department and they told me that if I didn't have someone on the grant application that had already done one, I'd have a very hard time securing it alone. I did apply to an SBIR grant through NASA. Luckily we had a team member who has submitted and received NASA grants to lead us through the process. It took about a week to put the required parts together. These applications are via web portal and have multiple sections and stages, so don't wait until the last minute to fill them out.

Bank Loans

If you have a brick and mortar store or a local small- to medium-sized business, a bank loan is something you should consider. Bank loans are typically used to expand an existing business, and they are very risk averse. Banks want to see previous cash flows and demonstration that you have the ability to deliver.

The great thing about a bank loan is that you get to keep your equity. The bad thing about a bank loan is the fact that you need to make fixed payments to the bank, and if you can't make said payments, your business will become bankrupt. The bank will then cease your company's assets and try to salvage what they can of their money. Overall, unless you have a successful business and are looking to expand capacity, I don't recommend this route.

In summary there are several alternative funding sources, the trick is to find out what is right for your business. If you have viral potential then go for crowd platforms. If you have a TV personality go for Shark Tank. If you are a scientist go for grants.

What I've Learned

In this chapter I'll be discussing mistakes I've made and the lessons I've learned from them, and I may even include one or two things I've done right. One key thing I've learned is that to build a great team you need to make sure that everyone fits in the company culture. Having everyone jive will make the tough and often stressful times much easier to manage.

Contractors

There will always be a need for lawyers, accountants, programmers, etc., so contractors are a necessity when operating a start-up. However, finding the right contractor, aligning incentives, defining milestones and when necessary managing that contractor is very important in achieving a positive outcome. I'm going to go over several scenarios that I hope you can draw insight from.

App Development

I've had good and bad experiences with app development contractors. One thing I know for sure is that I am a much better manager after taking an online course on iOS development. I encourage everyone to learn basic programming skills. One lesson to take away is that it is important that the bid be a flat rate contract for the entire job, not hourly.

I was raising funds for a venture and was engaging with an investor who pressured us to use this developer friend of his. The contractor refused to give us our code unless we signed a new contract that was over double the initial contract we signed. I had no choice but to sign the contract to get the code we had already spent $25,000 for. After I signed I told them we weren't going to pay them because (and this is an important distinction) they made me sign the contract amending the initial contract **under duress**. This means that because the app development firm was essentially extorting me, the contract I signed was void. I was able to remove the venture from legal liability to pay the firm and I was able to get our code. However, getting our money back ended up being expensive and time consuming. I believe that had I, the CEO, known more about app development, we could have potentially avoided this whole snafu.

Lawyers

Finding a good lawyer is critical. In my experience, try to find an independent lawyer or a small firm to do your work. Expect to pay between $250 to $500 per hour and about $1,000 for entity set up. If you don't know or can't find a lawyer you trust, go to a local accelerator program and ask them for a recommendation.

Finding a good patent attorney is especially important. I picked the wrong patent law firm once and spent more than $30,000 for a provisional patent. I also got a recommendation to an amazing patent attorney from an investor, converting the non-provisional and receiving the granted patent for less than $10,000.

I write most of my own contracts or edit boilerplate documents, but when it is important I have an attorney review my documents. I highly recommend having lawyers or at the very least an MBA with contracts experience review documents for you.

Patents

There are essentially two types of patents, a design patent and a utility patent, but there can be some overlap between the two types. Consider the BaziFIT device. We applied for a utility patent which we received three years after our submission. Our patent has claims that outline the way our sensor attaches to workout equipment and how the sensor works with our platform to measure user improvements and count reps. One part that we considered patenting is the way our sensor attaches to the equipment, but because we weren't sure at the time if our mechanism would change, we didn't patent it. If we had we would patent the design so no other product could use the same method to do the same thing.

Accountants

Same as with lawyers, I recommend working with small accountant firms or a single CPA. They will want to sell you on bookkeeping services but I'd recommend you keep your own books if you have any financial literacy and have the accountants do the taxes and audits.

Marketing

If you're a start-up, don't bother paying a marketing consultant. Any decent designer or web developer should know SEO marketing and how to position your social messaging. Don't be intimidated by online marketing. When your company is at an early stage, you or someone on your team can read up on it and do it internally.

Designer

I recommend getting a graphic designer to be permanent member of the team. Each designer has their own style and it is important that your design is consistent throughout your brand. Your logo, website, pitch deck, business card and any other visual assets need to have consistency, so having one head designer is critical. Up until I brought on our designer we weren't taken seriously, but once he revamped our website the impact was dramatic.

When to pay employees

When you're raising funds, investors will ask how long your runway is. A runway is essentially how long your funds will last before you take off (or go flying off the end of the runway). The key is understanding milestones and what resources you'll need to get to that point. A big killer of runway is if / when / how much to pay employees. When you're tight on resources you can't afford to pay much to your team. However, you must pay them something or they will spend time they could be working making ends meet. If you can find someone who is financially comfortable and has free time, don't pay them; save the money for someone else. Once you raise a series A or start making revenue you can begin paying people real money. The way I see it, $2,500 a month is what people need to survive in most start-up cities, $5,000 is comfortable and $8,000 when you're doing well.

More things I've learned:

Networking events

I have found that drinking is prevalent in networking. Because hangovers suck over 30 and I don't need the extra calories I generally don't partake as much any more. Now I stick to sipping even though most start-up events are open bar. If you're with a crowd drinking mixed drinks, I alternate between gin and tonic and straight tonic (they look the same). It isn't a bad thing to be a mostly sober person at these events; the phrase "loose lips sink ships" is true. I've seen many of the shenanigans that happen at the end of these events, so in addition to not imbibing to excess I also generally try to leave before the end.

Buying a house

If you can swing it, do it. You shouldn't put all of your money into your venture, having multiple investments is a good idea. I think of renting as throwing money away. Someone paying $1,500 a month for rent will spend $180,000 over 10 years.

Silicon Valley

Move away from the Bay; it isn't worth it. The Bay Area is absurdly expensive and oversaturated with highly capable people. I had moderate start-up experience compared with other start-up executives in the Bay Area, but in Boulder I am much more accomplished by comparison. I wouldn't have been able to buy a home or teach as an Adjunct Professor at a big university in the Bay Area like I've been able to in Boulder.

That being said, sometimes it can be easier to meet investors in the Bay, and going out there can help you rub elbows with the right people. Just know that living there is significantly more expensive than other places like Boulder, Austin or even the Boston area.

Dating and marriage

I'm lucky that I'm married to a brilliant woman who has her own career outside of the start-up world. If you're an entrepreneur I'd recommend dating or marrying someone with a stable income and career. As you know, or will soon find out, within any given week you can be doing great, then have a catastrophe, then be doing fantastic again. Having some stability is very helpful.

Personal time

It is very important to take a mental break from your venture. I'll work 12 to 14 hours a day sometimes and in order to stay sane I need breaks. These breaks aren't just for a coffee or a smoke; you need to find a way to take your mind off of what you're doing. Some people like video games, some people exercise, some people watch TV. I personally like to coach soccer. Three days a week I'm on the field teaching eight- and nine-year-olds that beautiful game. It's my Zen time. I completely lose track of my work issues and am in the moment; it charges my batteries.

It is also important to make sure you devote enough time and energy to your friends, family and significant other. They are your support network and it is critical that you don't forget that. I specifically devote time to call, text and spend time with my loved ones because as a founder you can become too focused on your venture, oftentimes to the detriment of your personal relationships. I make a conscious effort to cook dinner for my wife once a week and we take frequent trips together.

Equity

This is an important topic that has been covered at length in this handbook, but I wanted to leave you with a few final thoughts on it. When you're starting a company you have 100% of the equity. As you build your company, you'll need to give up equity either to capital (purchases and compensation) or to incentivize your team. I've found that most everyone is going to want to have as much equity as they can get, and many people won't be satisfied with what you give them. It is critically important to make sure the team members are happy and that you keep enough equity to get to the finish line. Think of equity as both a finite resource and a renewable resource, fueled by the pain of dilution. Just because someone is critical at one point of development doesn't mean they will be critical later, but any equity you give them they will own for the life of the entity. I've included a pie chart that demonstrates what I'd recommend targeting initially. If you can put capital to your first round you can keep control and raise funds. Most of the time the initial capital will be your own. Unfortunately, if you don't have personal wealth or a rich friend or family member, raising the initial funds is an epic uphill battle.

In the chart below you'll see a breakdown of the equity in a hypothetical post-seed round start-up. The founder started with 100% of the equity, then raised initial seed capital from friends and family and awarded them with equity. Then the founder had to build a team and create a prototype which was used to secure angel financing.

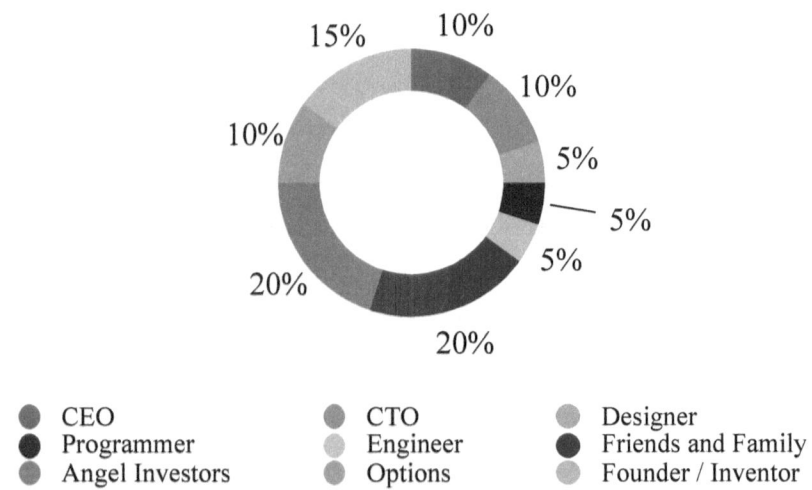

Note: If family invested the initial funds (and wished to vote the same way as the founder) the founder and their family would have a combined 35%, thus they would only need the vote of two or three team members for majority, meaning unless almost everyone on the team voted against the founder, they would have majority. Frankly, no founder should have absolute control over their company. It is important that there are checks and balances in corporate governance.

Mentor Whiplash

Throughout your journey in entrepreneurship you'll hopefully find mentors who are experienced entrepreneurs or business professionals that help you make the best decisions for your business. All the mentors I've known try to give the best possible guidance and advice to their mentees. Mentors are valuable because they draw from their wealth of experiences and let you know what they think the best course of action is.

The problem is that there are almost never two identical business scenarios, and there is often more than one right answer. Because of this, two equally experienced and respected mentors can give you conflicting advice. This poses a difficult scenario, especially for young entrepreneurs. I've noticed that many recent graduates are trained to think that there is a right and a wrong answer. But with start-ups there are often many right answers that could lead to success in different ways. The important thing to remember is to take the mentor's background into consideration. Mentors give advice based on their experiences, and those may or may not be applicable to the problem at hand.

For example: BaziFIT can be used effectively in both physical therapy and personal training markets. The product is a sensor that attaches to equipment to give feedback on the workout. An inexperienced entrepreneur may say, "Well, go for both markets!" That will most likely lead to failure because when you're fundraising or entering the market, focus is key. Because both surgeons and personal trainers liked our product, we turned to mentors to help advise us. Mentors from the consumer space (like Brad Feld of Foundry Group) recommended going into the consumer space and mentors form the medical space recommended going into the medical space.

Game Theory

I define game theory as the analysis of a scenario to manage risk and position yourself for the highest probability of success. The classic example is the prisoner's dilemma. Two individuals rob a bank, the cops catch both and have them in separate rooms. The cops give the two crooks the same options: If they both keep quiet they both walk away, if they both confess they both get 10 years, if one confesses and the other doesn't then the one who confesses receives one year and the other receives life in prison. What should they do?

Because the prisoners are only in control of what they personally say, they only have two options: talk or keep quiet. Talking becomes the best option because it allows for no more than a ten year sentence, while also guaranteeing you don't receive a life sentence. It's the safest bet.

I use game theory in every opportunity I can. I look at the options, identify the worse case scenario, then make a decision on whether the worse case is worth the best case scenario.

If you are ever trying to figure out an opponent's game theory breakdown, the first thing you identify is what they would want for a best case scenario and what would be their worse case scenario. You will also want to identify what resources they have, and use this information to theorize how they will use those resources to achieve their objectives.

However, worse case scenario is subjective. To some, being broke is their worse case so they would rather work a steady job that they may dislike rather than risk starting their own company. To others that mundane job is untenable and they would rather be broke than hate their job. I have friends who don't understand why I do start-ups instead of getting a stable, great paying job. Meanwhile, I question how they can keep going to their boring, steady humdrum job day in and day out. It's all about perspective.

I went to grad school because I absolutely hated my corporate job. I would rather have empty pockets while working on a start-up than be miserable working a nine-to-five. I want to benefit from my value, not create value for someone else.

Public Speaking

Public speaking is something that comes relatively easy for me, probably because I truly enjoy talking to everyone. I'd additionally credit Dave Ziegler, my high school debate coach, who helped me not only refine but also weaponize my speaking abilities. Debate was the most valuable class I took in high school, and much to my chagrin it has since been canceled at my alma mater because of budget cuts. It pains me that others will not be able to gain the skills I was able to in Debate.

If you want to look at it classically, there are three components to public speaking: ethos, pathos and logos. Ethos is the character of the speaker. Do you come off as professional, believable, confident? Pathos is the emotional appeal to the audience. Logos means logic, whether what you're saying is logical and accurate. The best speakers are good at all three of these areas.

Former President Barack Obama is an excellent example of an orator that excels at all three. He is confident, logical and passionate. He speaks very deliberately, making sure everyone listening is following what he's trying to say.

Some speakers are very good at two of the three and can still be very effective speakers. Another President, Donald Trump, while being widely viewed as lacking in the logos category, would score very highly in both ethos and pathos because of his unflappable nature, his likability to his base and his strong appeals to their emotions. To his fans he has the very best ethos. He is the billionaire on TV they are used to watching. He is very confident and looks the part. His speeches, while oftentimes factually inaccurate, ooze pathos. He is a very effective practitioner of using emotions to reach his audience.

If you aren't sure whether or not you're a good speaker, record yourself speaking. If you use intra-word pauses like "uhhh," "um" and "like" a lot, stop. Make the effort to end that bad habit. When you feel your mouth opening to say something like the former, stop and take a breath. Literally, take a large breath in when you feel your mouth opening. After your breath you should have time to figure out what you're going to say.

Asking the audience a rhetorical question or having them raise their hand is a good way to engage your audience at the beginning of your speech. It's also very important to understand what you're doing with your posture, as well as with your hands and legs. You don't want to sway, put your hands in your pockets, speak too softly, be monotone or speak too quickly. Some habits that will help include: Use of your hands to emphasize points, making good eye contact with people throughout the room, moving around in a slow, deliberate manner, using voice inflection to make points and making sure you change your cadence to emphasize your points. Engage with your audience when you have a chance, but don't ask the audience a question that you're not 100% sure of the answer.

Grad School

When I was picking grad schools I picked Clark University because of the small class sizes and the focus on teamwork rather than individual assignments. Pick a program that isn't just highly ranked, pick a program that will best fit your learning style. I'd recommend going to the AACSB website to find accredited programs.

I hope that you can learn from my experiences and avoid some of my pitfalls. I encourage you to speak with mentors and other experienced executives and see if they can share some more stories or gems of wisdom.

Going All In

Often times on your first venture, you will need to go all in. Meaning that you will need to leverage your savings and assets to be able to get your venture off the ground. Investors will appreciate the fact that you are committed to your project.

That being said, only put in what you can afford to lose. Putting a second or third mortgage on your house or personally guaranteeing a large amount of debt is risky and is probably not the best decision.

Exits

My mentor, Uncle Jeff, has been an entrepreneur basically his whole life. He has exited more than $500 million dollars over his multiple ventures. At one point he was a multi millionaire and was set for life. Instead of retiring he kept on rolling over his capital into the next venture, without setting some aside for a rainy day.

After having several unsuccessful ventures he became bankrupt. He is now rebuilding and will soon have a massive several hundred million dollar venture off the ground. The road ahead is always uncertain, so when you exit, save for that rainy day.

Entrepreneur's Checklist

Now that we've covered the content lets see if you're ready to dive into entrepreneurship. I've given you the tools, but only you can determine if you're ready.

When starting a business you will be pulled in a dozen different directions at the same time. These business duties will undoubtably take a toll on your personal life. Financially you will be stretched. Your loved ones will receive less of your time.

True, this is temporary and once things start going you will have more time and plenty of money from your growing venture. The truth is that most startups fail and the ones that do eventually succeed often take years to gain traction. There is a saying, what most people consider an overnight success is really a five year success.

Are you willing to devote years of your life to your vision? Are you willing to sacrifice your comfort for the pot of gold at the end of a rainbow? Are you willing to quit your job and work hundred hour weeks with no pay? Can you walk away after two years with just experience and be OK with it?

There have been dark times in my ventures. I've run out of runway and couldn't afford to pay myself or my team. I had to tell my team that I couldn't pay them the next month, and at the same time I had to motivate them to keep working on the project. I've spent some of my the last few dollars I had on gas to get me to meetings that led to nothing. There will be countless people who tell you no and it isn't easy to keep going. You need to choose to have the stick-to-itiveness (my favorite word) to keep moving forward. While at the same time knowing when to throw in the towel and start something new.

Whenever my wife and I go on a vacation, she makes a checklist of what we need for the trip. Here is a high level checklist of things you'll need to figure out in the beginning of your entrepreneurial journey.

Checklist

1. _____ Come up with your idea.

2. _____ Find your target customers and market size.

3. _____ Demonstrate product market fit by surveying and interviewing potential customers.

4. _____ Find a co-founder or build a team to join you on this venture.

5. _____ Put together your cap table and form your entity.

6. _____ Make a detailed plan to take you to an MVP (minimally viable product).

7. _____ Put your cash flow projections together and come up with a valuation.

8. _____ Finish your executive summary, pitch deck and get feedback from mentors.

9. _____ Secure resources to get you to an MVP.

10. _____ Produce your MVP.

11. _____ Make your first sale.

12. _____ Figure out the resources you'll need to scale.

Glossary

This is a glossary of common start-up terms. I'd consider this a good vocabulary list to study and become familiar with because you will probably encounter them in your entrepreneurial journey.

Term	Definition
Amortization	Similar to depreciation, amortization reduces the book value of the asset. In this case the asset is intangible and doesn't need to have a set life or length of use to the company.
Angel Investor	An individual investor that typically invests under $250,000. Most invest in early stage companies and have a higher risk tolerance than venture funds.
Asset	Something of value owned by the company, typically acquired by the company by a capital expenditure. If the asset only has value for a period of time, the asset's book value is depreciated over the life of the asset.
Book Value	The current value of an asset on your company's balance sheet.
Burn Rate	Similar to Runway, your burn rate is the monthly operating expenditures you incur.
Capital	Capital just means money. Other words with the same meaning include funds and cash.
Cap Table	Also known as a Capitalization Table, this document outlines the ownership of all the equity in a company.

Term	Definition
Cash Flows	The documentation of or a document that outlines your revenues, operating expenditures and capital expenditures. It tracks all of the money coming in and out of a venture.
Capital Expenditures	These are things a company spends money on that can be categorized as an asset, such as: vehicles, machines, buildings, land, patents, trademarks and inventory (until you sell it).
Cliff	The minimum time an employee needs to stay with the company in order to get any vesting equity. Say an employee is receiving 4% equity over a vesting schedule of two years. If there is a 12 month cliff and the employee leaves in month 11, they would walk away with nothing, rather than just under 2% if they stayed another month.
COGS	Cost of Goods Sold is what it costs you to produce the products you sell. It is typically a per unit calculation.
Competitors	Companies in an industry that provide the same or similar products or services to roughly the same market of consumers.
Customer Acquisition Cost	The cost it takes to gain a customer, which can include: search ads, referrals, social media marketing, sponsorships and all other advertising. You then divide your total advertising costs by the number of sales you had within a certain time period.
Common Shares	This is the default share type and typically given to early investors or founders. This type typically has better voting rights than preferred shares.

Term	Definition
Depreciation	The reduction of book value of an asset over time. If a machine you buy for $100,000 lasts 10 years you could do a straight line depreciation over 10 years. This would mean your book value of the asset in year two would be $90,000, and $10,000 in year 10.
Dilution	When a company has a full cap table and wants to raise another funding round they need to make new shares to sell to the new investors. This process is called dilution. Say a company has 2,000,000 shares and has a $2,000,000 valuation, so each share is worth $1. If they want to raise $500,000 they will need to issue and sell 500,000 new shares, so the company will now have 2,500,000 shares and be worth $2,500,000. If a founder has 100,000 shares equaling 5% (100,000/2,000,000) after the investment they would own 4% (100,000/2,500,000).
Duress	You can never force someone to sign a contract or amend a contract by threat. If you hired a developer who refused to give you the code you already paid him for unless you sign a new contract promising to pay them more, you would be asked to sign the contract under duress, making the contract void.
EBITDA	Earnings Before Interest Taxation Depreciation and Amortization, or what is left over after cost of goods sold (COGS) and operating expenditures but before you remove capital expenditures.
Equity	This refers to all of the shares, regardless of class, of a company.

Term	Definition
Exit	An exit is the sale of the company or any other liquidation event. A partial exit is possible if a merger occurs and the other entity purchases only a portion of the company.
Fiduciary Responsibly	If you are an executive of a startup you are legally obliged to do what is best for the company and its investors.
Focus Group	Market research typically performed in groups of 5 to 9 participants. The group is given some type of stimuli, such as watching a video, using an app or trying a product, and asked to give their feedback.
Gross	Referring to the total amount and not adjusting for any costs. Gross revenue is simply all of the revenue brought in by a company. Net revenues are gross revenues minus cost of goods sold (COGS).
IoT	Internet of thing refers to small sensors that are connected via the internet. This includes a wide range of devices and sensors that can collect data such as movement (Fit Bit), temperature (Nest), audio / video (Ring), ... etc.
Liability	A debt or obligation the company has to pay a person or entity. These include any non pre-paid services, unpaid wages and debt.
Market	A segment of the population that a company or industry focuses on to sell their products or services.
Mentor Whiplash	Having multiple accomplished mentors and advisors giving you contradictory advice. Know that mentors' advice is shaped by their experiences so take all the feedback you can and make your own decision.

Term	Definition
MVP	Minimally Viable Product or MVP refers to the most basic product or service you can offer to customers. New components are then added periodically after launch. Often a team will outline all of the features they want in a product or service, then prioritize the components from the most critical components to the most frivolous.
Net	Net refers to an adjusted gross. Net revenues would be gross revenues minus cost of goods sold. Gross revenues are all revenues brought into a company.
NPV	Stands for Net Present Value. This is the concept that a dollar in your hand now is worth more than the promise of $5 in five years. This calculation is done by applying a rate of discount to future cash flows, typically between 10% and 30%. $$\frac{\text{future cash flow}}{(1 + \text{interest rate})^{\text{time}}}$$
Operating Expenditures	These are costs that are used to run your business. They are things a company spends money on that cannot be categorized as an asset, such as salaries, utilities, office rent and insurance (once you use it, if you pre-pay and haven't used a service, you can categorize it as an asset).
Pivot	Changing a business strategy from its current course. This can include large changes in the product, go-to-market strategy or target market.

Term	Definition
Post-Money	The value of the company after the completion of an investment. If a company is selling 20% of its equity for $1,000,000, the post-money valuation is $5,000,000. The pre-money valuation would be $4,000,000.
Pre-Money	The value of a company prior to an investment. If a company is selling 20% of its equity for $1,000,000 the pre-money valuation is $4,000,000. The post-money valuation would be $5,000,000.
Preferred Shares	Typically given to investors, this class of shares has preferred pay back of dividends and receives funds first upon liquidation.
Product Market Fit	Making sure the product or service you're designing will be adopted by the specific market niche you've identified.
Profit	EBITDA minus capital expenditures, depreciation and taking amortization into account. Basically, revenues after all costs and taxes are removed.
Projections	Also known as pro-forma calculations, projections are just a projection of future cash flows. Using clearly defined assumptions, forecast your revenues, operating expenditures and capital expenditures. Projections are always wrong, the key is to clearly define your assumptions and be ready to defend them.

Term	Definition
Public Disclosure	Regarding patents, a public disclosure happens when an inventor or someone associated with the invention states publicly or publishes work on or about the novel aspects of the invention. If the public disclosure occurs, the inventor has one year to file a patent in the U.S. If no patent is filed the invention becomes public domain. European law only has a six month grace period.
Public Domain	Inventions or intellectual property that is in the public domain is free to use without having to receive rights from the patent holder. This can occur due to public disclosure of the technology or if the patents have expired. Sometimes companies, especially pharmaceutical companies, slightly modify something that is in the public domain and patent the modified invention.
Qualified Investor	When you're fundraising beyond friends and family, you can't solicit investment from non-qualified investors. The qualification may change over time so I recommend looking it up. Currently, a Qualified Investor has a net worth of more than $1,000,000 or an individual income of more than $200,000 per year.
Revenue	The money you bring in from sales of your product or service.
Restructuring	Sometimes things don't work out and you need to restructure your cap table. In this event the board and shareholders agree to amend or completely revise the cap table, bylaws and/or Articles of Incorporation.

Term	Definition
Round	A funding round is a capitalization of the company from an investment. Rounds are categorized in series that start off at pre-seed, then seed, then series A.
Runway	It is important to forecast your costs, the number of months you can manage your business is your runway. This is important for fundraising, you want to show your investors that you are asking for enough money to reach your goals.
SAAS	Software as a service can include any number of digital services targeted to either corporate or consumers.
SEO	Search Engine Optimization is the use of key words in your website's meta tags to raise your rank in search results.
Share Classes	The default share class is Common Shares, these are typically given to founders or early investors. Preferred Shares are typically given to investors. Common Shares are typically given more votes and Preferred Shares are given priority when issuing dividends and when a liquidity event occurs.
Substitutes	Unlike direct competitors, a substitute doesn't do exactly the same thing that you and your competitors do, substitutes do it in a different way. For example, if I'm looking to go on a trip from Denver to San Francisco I'd look to book a flight. Competitors in that industry are companies like United, American Airlines, Southwest and Delta. However, I don't need to fly, I could take a bus, train or drive from Denver to San Francisco. Substitutes in this case would be driving, Uber, Lyft, Amtrak and Greyhound.

Term	Definition
Survey	Done for market research to determine customer profile. Participants can be compensated or uncompensated; if the survey is short it is typically uncompensated. A short survey can be done in under 20 minutes and is typically less than 10/15 questions. Make sure each question is very clear and that you're not asking too much in one question.
Series	This is the categorization of funding rounds. The rounds are identified separately because each round has a different evaluation. Starting at pre-seed (concept) progressing to seed (prototype or first sales) then going into series A, series B, etc. that help the company scale.
Sweat Equity	Shares or equity given to a founder or early employee in exchange for their work.
Unlevered	Simply does not take debt into consideration. Thus, an unlevered free cash flow looks at cash flows prior to servicing debt.
Vesting	The schedule that an employee receives his or her equity compensation. The employee will receive the equity continuously, monthly or quarterly and it is usually prorated. If an employee is receiving 4% equity over a vesting schedule of two years, the employee will receive 1% every six months during the first two years. Also see "Cliff."

Acknowledgements

First of all, thank you Corrin Salamatian, I'm eternally grateful for your kindness, patience and exceptional editing skills. I'm very lucky to have you as my wife, and I'm not sure anyone else could have turned my chicken scratch into this full-fledged book.

Next, thank you Mom and Dad for your everlasting emotional and financial support through the tough times. You have always encouraged me throughout my successful and unsuccessful ventures and none of this would have been possible without the two of you.

Jeff Arsenych, thank you for everything you've helped me with, not to mention all of your help with the finance section. I would not be able to write this book without the decades of mentorship you have given me. Your entrepreneurial ventures inspire me, and it is an honor to be working shoulder to shoulder with you.

Andrew Miller, I really appreciate all your design help on this, and over the years. You always knock it out of the park. Great job on the cover!

Chris Porter, I appreciate you for helping me make the book more readable.

Finally, thank you to all my investors, friends and family who have supported me, encouraged me, inspired me, motivated me and who have taken the time to read earlier versions of this book to help me provide my readers with the best possible experience.

Author Bio

Tallis started his first venture in 2004, exiting that venture in 2007. Since then he has earned his **MBA** from Clark University's Graduate School of Business, taught at the University of Colorado's Leeds School of Business as an adjunct professor and been involved with more than a dozen ventures.

He has participated in ventures in artificial intelligence in stock training, machine learning algorithms for IoT, medical devices, pharmaceuticals, online platforms, consumer electronics, hospice service, music industry and now literature.

Throughout his ventures he has gained valuable experiences that he's been able to share with others through mentoring and teaching. Over the years of mentoring, he has seen new entrepreneurs struggle with some of the same issues. Tallis lives in Boulder, Colorado with his wife, Corrin, and their dog, Bella.

This photo and the back cover photo were taken by
Manuel Picar / Picar Production

Notes

www.ingramcontent.com/pod-product-compliance
Lightning Source LLC
Chambersburg PA
CBHW021442210526
45463CB00002B/617